Bygone Worksop

Michael J. Jackson

The Worksop Archaeological and Local Historical Society

ISBN-10   0-9501203-2-4
ISBN-13   978-0-9501203-2-4

Published by The Worksop Archaeological and Local Historical Society
Printed by Bayliss Printing Company Limited

CONTENTS

SUPPLEMENTARY ILLUSTRATIONS

ILLUSTRATIONS

Front Cover: The Top of Bridge Street
Frontispiece: Bridge Street/ Potter Street Corner

End piece: Walter and William
Bound for Church

Foreword.

This book completes a trilogy begun in 1969 with Worksop of Yesterday and continued in 1992 with Victorian Worksop. Like them, Bygone Worksop is mainly concerned with the town in the 19th century, though one article is wider in scope and another two deal with topics of a more recent date. Some provide additional information on themes included in the earlier books, several introduce new subjects while others tell of the lives of remarkable Worksop people, either well known in their own time or quite humble but with interesting stories to relate.

Even taken together, these three books make no claim to completeness. Fresh material is constantly coming to light. Since being written, several articles in this book have had to be modified to include recently discovered information. Our knowledge of bygone Worksop is constantly evolving. It could be that the recent archaeological work on the Romano British site at Gateford will completely alter our understanding of the area at that early stage of its history. A further example of change is taking place as I write these introductory words. Within the past fortnight a long familiar part of Worksop has disappeared. The Wesleyan Chapel, its ancillary buildings; the Wesleyan Day School (later Newcastle Street School) and two houses have been razed to the ground. These will be replaced, according to plans, by a modern complex containing a place of worship and both commercial and residential premises.

However, neither the discoveries at Gateford nor the memories of the chapel need to be altogether lost to the people of Worksop. The former has already been written up and published and the latter will be preserved in photographs, plans and the recorded recollections of those who knew it. A focal point for any public display of such material is a town museum and it is a great personal sadness, one shared by others in the town, that Worksop no longer has such a place where local artefacts, illustrations and ephemera can be exhibited for people to see. The peremptory closure of the museum means that objects already in store, together with anything that comes to light in the future – including the discoveries from the Gateford site – may never be displayed in the town.

I have been interested in Worksop's past for over fifty years and have found it an absorbing and fascinating study. It was first sparked at the long closed and demolished Lincoln Street and St. John's Boys' Schools and fostered by the acquaintance and friendship of many who knew the town, who were attracted by its past and whose hope was to perpetuate its story, its traditions and its people for future generations. This has also been the foremost aim of The Worksop Archaeological and Local Historical Society which has published this book and its predecessors, which delves into the town's past at its meetings and through the individual interests of its members. Several articles in Bygone Worksop were first prepared as talks for this local society.

Without the help of many people this book would never have been published and I gratefully acknowledge their assistance. Malcolm Dolby and Richard Allsopp, chairman and secretary of The Worksop Archaeological and Local Historical Society, have been of great encouragement, David Wheeler has transferred my typescript to computer disk, Harry and Lucy Richardson have been responsible for publicity and sales, and Audrey Johnson has read part of the text and commented helpfully on it. I am also grateful to Worksop Library and the Bassetlaw Museum, both for the facilities that I have used and for help in providing illustrations. These are acknowledged individually. Any with no such attribution are from my own collection. My personal gratitude is also due to all who have taken an active interest in the production of this book and those who have supported its publication by their encouragement.

A busy corner where Bridge Street and Potter Street meet. c. 1905

(Picture by permission of Eric Coddington)

Worksop: a Potted History.

In the late 1950's work began to clear part of Scratta Wood[1] of its trees and scrub and reclaim the land for agricultural use. As the work proceeded it revealed the base of a crudely built wall that enclosed an area roughly oval in shape and measuring about ninety six feet by seventy five. It was clearly man-made and of great antiquity. Subsequent excavation uncovered a few pieces of pottery, fragments of animal bone and part of a brooch. These finds and the general appearance of the site dated it to the late Iron Age/Romano British period. Other similar features were exposed during the construction of the Worksop by pass in 1986 while aerial photography has indicated that there might have been even more. Only limited archaeology was possible and the results were inconclusive. All that can be suggested is that at the beginning of the first millennium, a scattering of small walled enclosures was dotted over and close to the place where Worksop now stands. Some of them may have been occupied, others, perhaps, were no more than animal compounds. Life in such habitations was both hard and primitive.

Worksop was settled in Saxon times and it is likely that its first inhabitants built their homes either on or close to what is now known as Castle Hill. Later, the Norman lords of the manor erected a castle on the top of the hill. At first this was of timber though the initial watch tower may have been replaced by a stone keep. By the early years of the 16th century, neither stick nor stone remained standing and when this photograph was taken, around 1900, the hill was crowned with trees and was the venue for a popular annual rook shoot. (Photo, by permission of Richard Allsopp.)

Although the land was then part of the Roman empire, imperial power weighed but lightly on the Worksop area. The nearest villa sites were at Mansfield Woodhouse, Oldcoates and Southwell and the closest main highway was some eight miles distant. Casual archaeological finds do, however, suggest that Roman influence was not altogether lacking. Some years ago a buried hoard of Roman coins was found at Ranby while, more recently and much more tantalizingly, part of the side of a lead coffin was unearthed by a metal detectorist, at Gateford. Its decoration marks it as unmistakably Roman. Interesting as the find is, the questions that its discovery poses are of equal significance. If the original burial was local it would suggest the residence of someone of substance in these parts. If it was not it would be useful to know how such a heavy and bulky object came to be where it was found.

Questions rather than facts predominate in Worksop's story throughout the first millennium. What is known is that during that period a permanent settlement was established and it was given a name. The date is less certain. The best that can be suggested is that during Saxon times, perhaps as early as the 7th century, a small family group led by a man named Weorc, decided that somewhere on the sandstone bluff, later known as Castle Hill, and overlooking the valley of the River Ryton, would be a suitable place to set up their home.[2] The Saxon word for a valley was "hope" and this pre-fixed with Weorc gave the community its name Weorchope which, over the centuries, has evolved to its present day spelling.[3] Life in such a settlement was hard, uncomfortable; even squalid. The homesteads were little more than thatched huts and although some food was grown and a few domesticated animals kept, the main constituents of the cooking pot came from the surrounding "living larder" which teemed with game and wild fowl. Worksop is not mentioned in any surviving written records of the time and virtually nothing is known about it though place names suggest that it was not the only settlement in the district. Rayton, Kilton, Manton, Scofton, Osberton, Carburton and Carlton all have a Saxon sound to them and there were doubtless others. Though sparsely populated the region seemed quite extensively settled. What impact the 9th century incursions by the Danes had can only be surmised though they added such names as Ranby, Thoresby, Perlethorpe and Netherthorpe to the local landscape. A small, bronze leaf -shaped object, buried for centuries and revealed by a metal detectorist at Hannah Park, is archaeology's sole clue to life in Worksop during what, with some justification, are often known as the Dark Ages. The object is a distinctive form of strap end, dating from the 9th century.[4] It would be unwise, of course, to speculate too widely on the evidence of a single object which might be a stray and have no real association with the district but the possibilities that it suggests are, at least, interesting.

As the first millennium ran its course, Worksop was a middling sized settlement, far removed from the great events and the stirrings of national history. Soon, at least, it was to lose its anonymity. Twenty years after the Norman Conquest of 1066, a survey was made of the land, its findings recorded in what was subsequently known as the Domesday Book. There, in its pages, is the earliest written reference to Worksop, or

Werchesope as it is spelt. The purpose of the survey was to set down who owned the land and what it was worth. Today the book is invaluable as an aid to visualising what the country and its many townships were like almost a thousand years ago.

The entry for Worksop begins by stating that the pre-conquest owner was Elsi, a Saxon thane. His lands, for which he was taxed, extended over three carucates which was reckoned to be an area that three plough teams could cultivate in one year. After the Conquest the manor of Werchesope was granted by King William to Roger de Builli,[5] a powerful Norman lord who built and lived in Tickhill castle and founded the Benedictine Priory at Blyth. One carucate at Worksop formed Roger's personal estate: the remaining land was shared between the townsmen of whom there were twenty two sochmen, twenty four villeins and eight bordars. The former were virtually free men holding their land without feudal obligations to their lord. The villeins also held land though had to work a specific number of days each week on the lord's estate while the bordars worked most of the time for the lord and only had a small allocation of land. In all twenty two ploughs were used in cultivating the land which was laid out in large open fields. From this information it is reasonable to suggest a population of around two hundred. Not all the land was under the plough; there were seven acres of meadow and a long strip

The Priory Church has just celebrated its 900th anniversary. It was founded in 1103 as a monastery of the Augustinian Order. Known as Radford Priory, it continued until 1538 when, during the Dissolution of the Monasteries, it was closed. Although most of the purely monastic buildings were demolished, the nave survived to be used as the parish church. For almost 400 years it remained incomplete until 20th century restoration brought it back to its original size and layout. This photograph was taken around 1910.

of woodland upon which the local pigs could root and graze. The entry concludes by stating that Worksop was valued at £8 before the conquest; twenty years later at the time of the survey it was one pound less which gives the impression that it suffered no great depredations at the hands of the invading Normans.

In the years that followed two significant additions were made to the town's appearance: one was a castle, the other a magnificent church. Of the former, nothing structural survives and known written references are scanty. What does remain, however, is Castle Hill, its man-made earthworks clearly resembling those of a motte and bailey castle. There is little doubt that all the original buildings were of timber; a watch tower on the motte, living quarters, stables and other necessary service facilities within the bailey or courtyard, all surrounded by a tall palisade. It could be that parts of the castle, the tower or keep, in particular, may have been replaced by stone but this is by no means sure. Whatever its story, it seems that its existence was short. It has survived longer in tradition than in visible ruins. By the early 16th century, though the hill remained, all signs of buildings had completely disappeared, it was, "clene downe and scant knowen wher it was," as one visitor to the town wrote in 1540[6]. Despite the little that is known about the castle, one fact can be stated with some certainty. No secret tunnels led from it, either to the Priory or anywhere else.

Following the death of Roger de Builli, the lordship of the Manor of Worksop passed to William de Lovetot whose principal residence was at Sheffield. Though somewhat distant from the town, he was responsible for a building, part of which has survived the centuries and today stands as Worksop's architectural treasure. In 1103 he founded and endowed a priory of the Augustinian order, dedicated at first to Saint Cuthbert and later, jointly, to that saint and Saint Mary. It stood some half a mile to the east of Worksop and was known as Radford Priory. Soon a small settlement began to grow around its gate with the present day Low Town Street as its main street and Abbey Street[7] and Aldred Street on the line of its back lanes. Radford developed as a twin township with Worksop, its name surviving until the end of the 19th century when it was still used in the census returns. The Boundary Inn on Potter Street traditionally marks the dividing point between the two communities.

The building of the priory was slow and it did not attain its fullest extent until well into the 14th century. First of all the recently completed small Norman church was either re-built or incorporated into a more fitting edifice for monastic worship. Over the years it was enlarged and embellished in the evolving architectural styles of the day while, around it, the necessary conventual buildings; the chapter house, dormitory, refectory, cloisters and prior's lodging, covered a considerable area. Finally, to complement all that had been done, the magnificent gatehouse was completed some two hundred years after the first stone of the priory was laid. Despite its size and splendour Radford Priory was never ranked as more than a medium sized house. As such, upwards of twenty monks[8] lived there, their days made up of worship and prayer, of looking after the property and estates with which their house had been endowed, providing hospitality for travellers, tending the sick and, perhaps, holding a school for a few local boys. Additionally they had a corn mill, probably a maltings and, among the crops that they grew, was liquorice.[9]

This continued to be cultivated in the town long after the priory had been closed and, especially in the 17th century, brought it no little notice. Among all this activity John Tickhill who served as prior between 1303 and 1313 quietly and painstakingly was responsible for the production of a masterpiece. Writing on sheets of vellum, he copied out the Book of Psalms, embellishing the script with delicately worked gilding. Subsequently the margins and capital letters were enhanced with richly coloured decorative patterns and the text illuminated with over four hundred cameo illustrations that glow like jewels from the page. Many of them depict incidents from the life of the biblical King David. This book, known as the Tickhill Psalter, is now one of the treasures of the New York library.[10] Whether this was the only such product of the scriptorium at Worksop will now never be known though it would be good to think that there were other books of similar excellence and that John Tickhill was able to pass on his skills to the following generation.

A PORTION OF THE OLD SHIP INN, 1875.

Throughout the Middle Ages and well into the 17th century virtually all the houses in Worksop were of timber framed construction with walls of wattle and dried mud. Signs of this still survive though most are hidden by later alterations. The Old Ship Inn is the most obvious example, where, despite modifications, it still has the appearance of a large town house of 16th/17th centuries. Its original appearance is even more apparent in this sketch of 1875, before it was cleaned up and re-furbished.

The Lordship of the Manor of Worksop, originally vested in Roger de Builli, passed, usually through the female line, to the Lovetots, the Furnivals and the Talbots, later to be the Earls of Shrewsbury. Not much is known of these men. In 1219 Sir Gerald de Furnival died in Jerusalem while on the 3rd. Crusade and his son Thomas similarly perished. On this second occasion the widowed mother, Maude de Furnival, sent her younger son, Gerald, to the Holy Land to bring back the heart of his brother for burial in the Priory church. Whether any local men followed their lords to Palestine is not known though it is likely. Three mutilated effigies in the church are silent reminders of Worksop's ancient lords; a fourth has a more illustrious memorial. He was John Talbot, first Earl of

Shrewsbury, and was mentioned by William Shakespeare in his play King Henry VI, part 1 where, for his bravery in the war against France under Joan of Arc, he is described as, "the great Alcides of the field, the valiant Lord Talbot, Earl of Shrewsbury."[11] He had come into his Worksop property on his marriage to a later Maude de Furnival.   She, so it was said, was as devout as he was brave and liked to spend her time in the upper room of the gatehouse, engaged in learned discussion with the monks or looking down onto the haggling throng of townspeople at the stalls set out around the market cross below. Following her death, and as a memorial to his wife, so it is thought, the earl ordered the porch to be built that stands to the east side of the front of the building and leads to the little known but delicately proportioned pilgrims' shrine.[12]

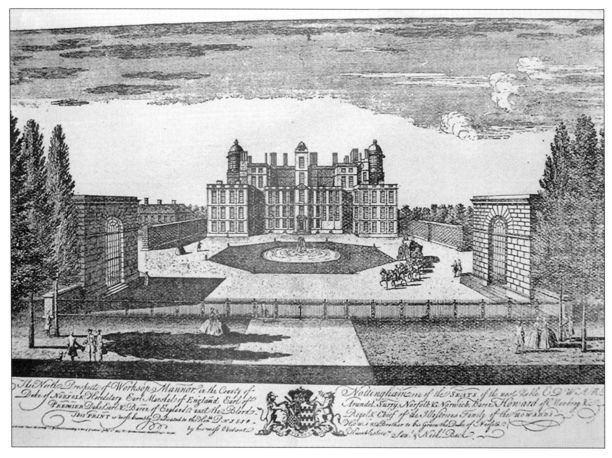

Nothing is known of the manor houses of medieval Worksop.   This is not so of their replacement of late Tudor times when Robert Smythson, pre-eminent architect of the period, built a residence for the 6th Earl of Shrewsbury that had few, if any, equals in the land.   This later illustration fails to do it full justice.   It was a tall building, its corner turrets pointing skyward and its multi-windowed walls dazzling in the sunlight and blazing with light in the darkness.   Sadly it was destroyed by fire in 1761.

Worksop formed but part of the estate of its medieval lords of the manor and their residence there would only have been occasional. Nevertheless, there must have been some fitting building for their use. Doubtless the castle would serve for the early Lovetots but their successors were more likely to have occupied a sequence of halls or manor houses. Of their location and appearance nothing is known, though it is likely that they were of stone. Whether any of them were built on Castle Hill or were predecessors of the great Elizabethan Worksop Manor is a matter of speculation. What can be said is that following the first millennium and throughout the Middle Ages, the priory and the castle or manor house dominated the twin townships of Worksop and Radford. No other building compared with them in size, appearance or solidity of structure. Of the rest, the houses, the out buildings, the places of work; all were basically of timber, mud and thatch, materials that were vulnerable to fire and storm. While most of these were small, little more than huts a few, as the years slipped by, were larger, perhaps containing several rooms. A street pattern was becoming apparent too. Already some of these houses lined what was later to be called Bridge Street while a few more marked the course of the future Potter Street. These two streets formed the nucleus from which Worksop was to grow. Throughout the years, visitors noted that it was a town of two principal streets and the scanty evidence that has survived suggests that these were they. Newgate Street is also of some antiquity and may have had its beginnings as a back lane to Potter Street. The latter, or Potter Gate as it was known in earlier times, led directly to Radford and it was along this road that from 1296 Worksop people made their way to the weekly Wednesday market and the annual fair. That Radford was the location of both church and market must have given it some status though it never seems to have seriously rivalled Worksop either in size or importance. Population is difficult to assess. Occasional tax returns record the number of householders who paid but take no account of those who were ineligible and, indeed, those who evaded payment. All that can be suggested is that there was some steady increase up to 1348 when the Black Death claimed up to one third of the inhabitants. Most worked on the land, a few may have been smiths of one sort or another, some woven cloth might have been produced while, later in the period one or two could have branched out as traders or merchants.

Little, if anything, that happened in medieval Worksop has been written on the pages of national history. Apart from its lords and its priors, few of the names of its inhabitants have survived the centuries and, of its buildings, only the nave of its monastic church and the gatehouse are still standing.

More certainty comes in with the Tudors. One event, at least, can be chronicled in some detail. This was the closure of Worksop Priory. In 1539 as part of the Dissolution of the Monasteries, Thomas Stokes, the prior, and the fifteen monks were pensioned off and sent packing. The buildings were despoiled of their valuables and all save the nave and west towers of the church and the gatehouse reduced to ruins. These provided the townspeople with a handy quarry and stones that were once part of the conventual buildings of the priory soon began to appear in houses, barns and boundary walls bereft of the monastic chancel, the nave stood open to the weather at its east end; a chilly place to gather for worship when the wind blew from that direction. Meanwhile, all the priory property and land in the town passed to Francis, 5th Earl of Shrewsbury, already Lord of the Manor.

Whatever residence the Earl might have had in the town was soon deemed inadequate for so vast an estate and, in the 1580's, a more fitting edifice was built. It was designed by Robert Smythson, the pre-eminent architect of the Elizabethan age. Hardwick Hall is a surviving example of his work. At Worksop, the manor that he built was tall, crowned with domed turrets, its walls lightened by many windows. Situated on rising ground, it was a magnificent building at any time, but at night, with lights shining from its myriad windows it glowed like a giant lantern. On a smaller scale and plainer in design, though still a striking building, Manor Lodge dates from the same time. Much altered over the years, its original purpose isn't clear. It might have been a hunting lodge. While not rivalling the work of the masons in the Manor Park, builders were busy in the town too. More compact, two storied timber framed houses were replacing some of the rambling structures of medieval times. The Old Ship could have been one of them and there were others. John Leland who passed through the town in the 1540's noted that it was, "A praty market of 2 streates and metely well buildid."

Splendid as the new manor looked, not all its early occupants found its accommodation to their liking. Mary, Queen of Scots certainly didn't. In the custody of the Earl of Shrewsbury, she was brought there in the summer of 1583 and spent several weeks confined in "a wretched bed chamber." This might be a reflection on the unfinished state of the manor while Mary was there, though of course, to a prisoner, no room would hold any attraction. Her son, on his accession to the English throne as James I, was certainly afforded more generous hospitality when he spent the night there on his journey from Scotland to London. No expense was spared. After hunting in the park, so it is recorded, "At last he went into the house where he was nobly received, with superfluity of all things that still every entertainment seemed to exceed (the) other. In this place beside the abundance of all provision and delicacie there was most excellent soul-ravishing musique, wherewith his highness was not a little delighted." So lavish was the hospitality that after the king had departed on the following day the people of Worksop were invited to take their pick of all that remained.

The number who might have taken advantage of the earl's bounty is not known as there is no record of the population. At best, an approximate figure can be calculated from the number of burials and baptisms listed in the parish registers. For the end of the 16th century this suggests that there might have been between seven hundred and a thousand people living in the town.[13] This would further indicate that the township was made up of one hundred and fifty to two hundred homesteads; certainly not a village but a middling sized market town. Growth was steady rather than pronounced during the first half of the 17th century. By 1650 the population had risen to around one thousand two hundred though by 1700 it was little different.[14] Fortunately these imprecise figures can be fleshed out a little as, in 1636, a detailed inspection was made of the town.

By then the Lordship of the Manor had passed through marriage to the Earl of Arundel and Surrey and he it was who commissioned John Harrison to survey his property in and

BEARDS MILL

This building was Worksop's first true factory. It was built in the late 18th century as a textile mill but the venture failed and it was converted to grind corn. Of its various owners, the best known was Mr. Joseph Beard, after whom it was named. For many years it was a water mill and the dam, which supplied its source of power was a popular leisure amenity in the town. In 1985 the mill was demolished to make way for the Mansfield Road roundabout on the bypass.

around Worksop. He made a very thorough job of it and by careful study it is possible to deduce the layout and extent of the town.[15] Here the briefest of summaries must suffice. Not surprisingly he gives prominence to the manor, "a very stately house .. .. build of freestone, being very pleasantly situated upon a hill, with gardens corresponding to the same." It was set in a park that was over seven and a half miles in circumference and contained more than two thousand, three hundred acres. The survey and other contemporary documents mention the names of one hundred and eighty people living in the town. This suggests a population of around a thousand though some of the very poorest may not have been included. Their homes ranged from one roomed hovels to quite substantial houses. The largest, described as an "inn or tenement" on Long Wall Way (Cheapside, Retford Road) contained seven rooms Next in size was Jesus House which had six rooms and was the home of Henry Cole. He was a substantial farmer who had more than two hundred acres under the plough and whose flocks grazed the Manton sheepwalk which spread over nine hundred and twenty four acres. Jesus House, probably an outbuilding of the Priory in origin, survived to the early years of the 20th century when, long neglected and semi-ruinous, it was demolished. Close by was a small cluster of buildings that were predecessors of Worksop's basic industries of later years. One was Bracebridge mill, a corn grinding water mill - one of three in the town- and the other was a kiln and malthouse. With but few exceptions all the buildings whether large or small were of timber frame construction and it would be fair to assume that they were thatched. Just a little stone was used, some of it filched from the Priory ruins, some quarried from the west of the town near Steetley. One building all of stone, and it was a rarity, was Manor mill which stood close to Castle Hill and was powered by a meandering tributary of the Ryton.

Of manufacturing industry there was none though the presence of a dye house and a tenter green where lengths of cloth were stretched out to dry suggests that some spinning and weaving took place in people's homes. A handful of workshops, too, provided other basic necessities. Two blacksmiths, a locksmith and nailmaker, a saddler, two sawyers and a joiner, two masons, a brewer and a charcoal maker are mentioned. Otherwise, most people's livelihoods came from the land. There were some large farms but most of the holdings were small, no more than a close of arable land with common grazing rights. Generally, most of the land close to the river and prone to flooding was used as meadow, the slightly higher ground was cultivated while the outer parts of the township were pasture. The largest of these was the Manton sheepwalk. While mixed farming predominated, one crop in particular was rather special. This was liquorice. It doesn't seem to have been extensively grown, just six small "liquorice gardens" are noted in John Harrison's survey but he does mention it in his introduction, "I cannot here omit that thing wherein this towne of Workesoppe excelleth all others with in this Realms & most noted for; I mean the store of Licoras that groweth therein & that of the best." Some of the crop was even sent to London.[16]

Choice in shopping in 17th century Worksop was not great as only five are recorded though this must be regarded as a minimum. One of them was the shambles and, additionally, some of the craftsmen would sell at the door without keeping a shop. Four stalls are also noted though whether they were in everyday use or just set up for the weekly market is not clear. Inns seemed similarly thin on the ground and there must have been more than the one or two that were included. The George was certainly in business for, twenty years later following its destruction by fire, it was described as, "tyme out of minde a victualling house."[17]

By 1636, the year in which John Harrison compiled his survey, life in Worksop had been ruffled by recent religious rumblings and was soon to be stirred, but lightly, by the upheavals of civil war. Around the turn of the century North Nottinghamshire was the centre of an extreme form of Puritanism. While most such people were content to strive to reform the Church of England from within, a minority felt that more drastic action was necessary. Known as Separatists, their aim was to break away from the established church and, contrary to the law of the times, follow their own form of worship. This ambition was to cause some of them to leave their own land, first to Holland and then to North America and to be known in history as the Pilgrim Fathers. Locally centred on Babworth and Scrooby, their influence radiated throughout the district and reached Worksop. The vicar, the Revd. Richard Bernard,[18] was so affected by their beliefs that, for a short time, he set up a Separatist church within the walls of the Priory itself and was supported by a hundred of his congregation. So great a defection brought down the wrath of the Archbishop of York on Bernard who recanted of his non-conformity and returned to more orthodox ways. His flock followed his example: no Worksop people sailed on the "Mayflower."

During the 18th century the appearance of Worksop began to take on a new look as brick replaced timber and daub as the most commonly used building material. Many of the new and rebuilt properties were constructed in the symmetrical Georgian style which gave the main streets an elegance that they didn't previously possess. This is apparent in this picture of Potter Street, even though the buildings have been neglected and were soon to be demolished.

No major action of the Civil War took place in or near Worksop though, with Welbeck Abbey garrisoned for the king and both Newark and Nottingham under siege, it would be surprising if the townspeople were not made aware of the conflict from time to time. They may possibly have heard about a skirmish near Thorpe Salvin when a party of Royalists from Welbeck was put to flight by a detachment of Parliamentarian cavalry. There might even have been a skirmish in the town itself though no details have survived. The sole evidence is three entries in the churchwardens' accounts which record the burial of six soldiers, five of whom were, "slaine in the towne." So few casualties suggest occasional clashes between foraging parties or patrols rather than a pitched battle.

Worksop, at the beginning of the 18th century was little different in population and appearance from what it had been a hundred years earlier. As the century ran its course it was to change in both these respects. In 1743 a visitation return made for the Archbishop of York recorded three hundred and fifty eight families in the town. This suggests a population of around fifteen hundred. By 1801 it had more than doubled to three thousand, two hundred and ninety one. This increase showed itself in the street plan of the town as it began to push out from its medieval layout. Not only were there more buildings and new streets but the whole appearance of the town began to change. This was due to the use of a new material. Most of the new houses were of brick, some of those already standing were re-fronted with brick and others, while retaining their timber framework, had their wattle and daub infilling replaced by brick. Although some thatch remained until well into the 19th century, all the new property and much of the old were roofed with pantiles. Not only were brick and tile less prone to fire than timber and thatch but they also gave the two principal streets a touch of elegance that was apparent until comparatively recent times.

An exception to this, one of the largest and most imposing 18th century town houses was built of stone. This still stands on the north side of Potter Street. It was the home of Henry Dunstan who, in 1745, was sufficiently highly regarded to serve as High Sheriff of the county. More professional men were practising in the town, too. Both doctors and lawyers were resident and others, as their work demanded, stayed for shorter periods. It was perhaps ironic that while some of the houses in the town were given a more substantial and pleasing look, one that had possessed those qualities for close on two hundred years was completely destroyed. This was Worksop Manor. By 1761 its ownership had passed to the ninth Duke of Norfolk who ordered extensive renovations to its interior. Just as these were virtually complete, the building caught fire and was razed to the ground. The Duke immediately commissioned James Paine, an eminent architect of the time, to prepare plans for its replacement. This would have been the largest country house in the land. Work proceeded apace until the Duke's heir died when it ceased, never to be re-started. Even so, one wing had been finished, a vast building in itself though only a quarter of the intended house

Meanwhile, at the northern end of the town, construction of a different sort was in progress. Men were at work on the Chesterfield Canal that was to link that town to the River Trent at West Stockwith. In 1777 it was complete and open to traffic by horse drawn narrow boat. One result of this was immediate. The price of coal, previously delivered from colliery to town by road, fell from 8d. (3.5p) to 4d. (1.5p) a hundredweight. Other consequences were more gradual. Following its opening, new buildings were attracted to its bank sides and to the northern end of the town. Many were functional such as a cluster of maltkilns that took advantage of the new form of transport but there were houses as well. Where previously a few isolated cottages dotted the landscape, new streets began to push out into hitherto open countryside. Eastgate was one of these, encroaching on what had previously been known as the Common. New working opportunities were created too. A handful of local men became boatmen, a few others found employment as lock keepers and the like while the Revd. John Peacock, curate at the Priory Church, as well as his church duties and being the "Master of a Public School" in his home at Jesus House, was also the first paymaster of the canal company. Just after the coming of the canal, an attempt was made to introduce manufacturing industry into the town. Following the destruction by fire in 1792 of his textile mill at Cuckney, William Toplis transferred his interest to Worksop. Two mills were built, one on the south side of the canal on Bridge Place, the other, probably on Mansfield Road, known to later generations as Beard's Mill.[19] Absolute certainty is difficult as written evidence is scanty for, within three years, both mills had closed. Various reasons for their failure have been suggested. Both the spinning of worsted and cotton were attempted as well as, "weaving filleting, turkey - stuff, sashes etc." Perhaps such ambitious expectations exceeded the technology of the day or competition may have been too great. Whatever the reason, the mills soon closed and were adapted to corn milling. The one by the canal, worked for many years in the 19th century by the Mapson family was, from its earliest days if not from its beginning, powered by a steam engine, certainly the first in Worksop. The birth on the 25th December, 1777 in the town of T.C. Hofland, later to become a well known landscape artist, may possibly reflect on this. His father, described as, "a rich manufacturer of cotton Mill machinery,"[20] could well have been responsible for fitting out the Worksop mills and, indeed, installing a steam engine in one of them. Failure as it was, this attempt to bring industry to the town did, at least, provide it with two substantial buildings as well as its first planned street. This was Norfolk Street with its sixty dwellings built as housing for the families who, it was anticipated, would be needed to work at the mills. Solidly built of local stone, the cottages are now occupied as individual houses but there are indications that they were originally planned as flats. Similar accommodation at Cuckney, provided by the same firm, certainly was. Some years ago a man who grew up in Norfolk Street had childhood memories of a kitchen range in his bedroom which suggests the same arrangement pertained here. The street still stands, outwardly little altered, the sole survivor of the first attempt to bring factory based industry to the town.

Impressions of 18th century Worksop are few and some are far from complimentary. In 1780 John Wesley rode into town and, on a scorching hot day, addressed a small gathering on Lead Hill. His reception was not encouraging. He was heckled, even pelted and later, in his journal, he castigated his audience as, "only a small company of as stupid people as ever I saw." It was not an auspicious start yet it led to the establishment of a Wesleyan society in the town which is still in being today. Nine years later, in June of 1789, Colonel John Byng paid an overnight visit. He was not impressed though it was his accommodation rather than the place that provoked his wrath. He stayed at the Red Lion, "a paltry looking inn," where he dined badly on, "stewed mutton chops and pickled salmon" and slept indifferently, "upon a sweltering feather bed with a straw kind of mattress." However, he admitted that the town was a "good station" and noted that the canal brought coal into the town at eight shillings (40p) a ton. "Happy purchase!" was his comment on that. He also admired the exterior of the Priory Church and explored the gatehouse where, to his surprise, he disturbed a school at work in the large upper room. But it was the Red Lion that provided his lasting memory and he returned to it in his final remark. "Nothing can have been nastier than our inn at Worksop; with ill cooking, stinking feather beds, and a conceited fool of a landlady: .. .. ". Whether such criticism was justified or whether Colonel Byng was difficult to please will never be known. What is certain is that during the 19th century, the Red Lion became widely regarded as the principal hostelry of the town and many testimonies exist to its hospitality.

For Worksop that century was to be one of change. The population increased almost fivefold from 3,291 to 16,455, new houses filled empty spaces within the town and pushed out into the surrounding countryside while machine made brick and slate transformed its appearance. The work pattern altered too. At the beginning of the century most men worked on local farms, by its end the majority were miners. The traditional occupations of malting, milling and timber working still provided some employment but their demands were small compared with the number who worked down the pit. Though still a market town in size, appearance and atmosphere, Worksop more and more became a place where the factory was replacing the farm, where the works' buzzer rather than the position of the sun regulated the day.

For centuries local government within the town had hardly changed. It was still centred on the meetings of the parish vestry, the magistrates and an archaic body known as the Court Leet. Between them they appointed such officials as the overseers of the highways and the poor, the constable, the pinder, the town crier and other minor functionaries. Such a haphazard system might have coped when the population was small but it was clearly inadequate when it numbered several thousands. Improvement came in 1852 when Worksop elected its first Local Board of Health which was, in all but name, a town council of nine members. After initial teething problems and under the forceful chairmanship of Joseph Garside, it provided the town with an efficient system of drainage and sewage disposal. This was its greatest achievement in its comparatively short existence for in 1894 it was replaced by an Urban District Council. This, too, functioned but briefly as, in 1931 Worksop was granted borough status and entitled to elect a town council.[21]

Although the horse remained the principal means of transport throughout the century its supremacy was challenged by the end. Few would have thought when, early on the morning of the 16th July, 1849, the first railway train pulled into the recently built station, that a new era of travel was beginning. Journeys that had previously taken days were reduced to hours, local people could visit family and friends countrywide, the products of mine, kiln and workshop were transported over a far greater area. The benefits of the railway were obvious and yet the people of Worksop seemed reluctant to acknowledge them. Travel in the early open carriages was uncomfortable and could be dangerous, punctuality was poor, connections with trains at Retford were inconvenient, the station was smoke and soot begrimed and only cleaned when a royal visitor was expected. Such were the complaints at the service provided by the Manchester, Sheffield and Lincolnshire Railway. One wit said that its initial letters stood for "Mucky, Slow and

By the early years of the 19th century, the Priory Church was in a parlous condition. After centuries of neglect, cracks appeared in the towers, the south wall was leaning dangerously out of true and other defects made the building unsafe for use. Extensive repair work was put in hand and this remarkable and rare picture shows it in progress. By 1845 sufficient had been accomplished to ensure the preservation of Worksop's oldest and most treasured building. (Picture by permission of Mr. and Mrs. F. Greaves.)

Late" and many in Worksop would have agreed with that. Despite such criticisms, the railways provided a means of mobility hitherto unknown. Without them it is doubtful if the well known townsman, Mr. George Gregg, would have been able to visit the Great Exhibition in London in 1851 and it is certain that the local pea crop would not have been served in the capital city's hotels within twenty four hours of picking.

Another new mode of transport, less prominent and certainly less chronicled than the railways, had a marked effect on people's lives. This was the bicycle, "almost as necessary," according to one person, "as a pair of boots." This was an exaggeration as new machines were not cheap. Worksop manufacturer George Vardy charged eight guineas (£8.40) for his Dukeries model. However, by the end of the century there were a good number on local roads, giving their riders a mobility comparable with that of horse owners. Apart from the obvious advantage of going to and from work, the bicycle opened up the possibility of new leisure time activities. In 1878 the Worksop Cycling Club was formed for those who enjoyed exploring the surrounding countryside while, in the first decade of the 20th century, catering for a similar need, G.H. Stancer, himself a keen cyclist, produced a neat little guide book, "Wheelmarks Round Worksop." Speedsters were not forgotten either as, from 1880, cycle races were included in the annual Whit. Monday sports day organised by the cricket club. Only an occasional car raised the dust on the streets until the final year of 19th century Worksop. Then, on the 11th May, 1900 upwards of fifty of them that were taking part in a rally, paused briefly outside the Lion Hotel while their drivers took breakfast within.

For most people, Sunday was a day of rest from normal work and one on which a good number of them attended services at church or chapel. This was less than tradition would have it though substantially more than attend today. According to a survey taken in 1851 around 3,500 out of a population of 7,215 were present at one service or other. This can be a little misleading as it does not take account of those who attended more than once or, indeed, those who were deterred from leaving home by a sudden thunder storm that broke just as they might normally be setting out for evening service. Choice was reasonably wide. For Anglicans, the Priory Church was ever present and was joined in 1869 by St. John's while, from 1884, a small group met in a mission room on Lead Hill prior to the building of St. Anne's in 1912. Methodism was represented by three distinct denominations, the Wesleyans, the Primitive Methodists and the United Methodists, the latter undergoing a number of name changes in its early years. Another denomination to change its name during the century was the Independents. They were later known as Congregationalists. While maintaining regular worship, providing most of the town's schools and arranging a wide variety of welfare and social activities, all the town's churches and chapels undertook major building projects and struggled to meet the financial demands that these brought about.

Centuries of neglect had left the priory Church in such a parlous state that radical restoration was vital. This was carried out during the 1840's. The four non-conformist churches had all built places of worship by the 1830's. All were on the small side and of modest appearance. Their inadequacies in accommodation and construction soon became apparent. In 1863 the Wesleyans opened their new chapel on Newcastle Street, some fifty yards from where its predecessor had stood. The others soon followed and the 1870's was a great decade of chapel building in Worksop. First off the mark were the United Methodists who, in 1875 built a new chapel on the site of their old one on Potter Street. The Congregationalists followed soon after. They had long been dissatisfied both with the location and the surroundings of their Westgate chapel and in 1876 moved to new and more prominently sited premises on Bridge Place. Three years later building work began on a new chapel for the Primitive Methodists. This was at some distance from their Newgate Street chapel and away from the main streets so favoured by the other denominations. They chose to build amid the new houses that were springing up to the north west of the town and were mainly occupied by mining families. When completed in 1880 it crowned the gentle rise of John Street. One hundred years later, not one of these 19th century chapels was still standing though two, those of the Wesleyans and the Congregationalists, now the United Reformed Church, have been replaced. To complete this brief survey, the Roman Catholics quietly established themselves on Park Street in 1840 while, in 1881, to the beat of drum and hearty singing, the Salvation Army marched into town.

1931 was an important year in the town's history as it was then granted borough status, an event celebrated on Charter Day when members of the newly elected council led a procession along the main streets to the Market Place. Here the Charter of Incorporation was handed to Councillor F.C. Foster, Worksop's first mayor. He is seen on the right of the front row of the parade, as it passes the Congregational Chapel on Bridge Place. Next to him is Mr. Malcolm MacDonald, M.P. for Bassetlaw while Mr. G.H. Featherstone, the town clerk, is on the left.

As well as houses, which increased in number by the hundred, a church and chapels, some buildings of both usefulness and prominence were added to the townscape during Victorian times. One of these was the Corn Exchange, opened in 1851 and still standing at the top of Potter Street. Although farmers did haggle there over the price of their crops on market days it served many other purposes. The magistrates' court met there, the Mechanics' Institute occupied two of its rooms at the back while the first floor assembly room was the venue for balls, meetings, bazaars and entertainments. It was the social centre of the town. In 1882 its ownership passed from a private company to the Local Board of Health. This brought about a change in name and the building soon became known as the Town Hall. Built about the same time, the Steetley stone and the glazed canopy of the railway station sparkled in the July sunshine as the first train drew into its platform in 1849. More decorative in design than the other stations on the line, it perhaps owed that distinction to anticipated patronage by the great families of the Dukeries and, their visitors. A third building, now sadly derelict, was the pumping station of the sewage disposal works. When it was opened in 1881 it marked the climax of over twenty years work to drain and cleanse the town. Standing just off Bracebridge, the building could not fail to attract the eye. Highly decorative, its tall chimney looked as if it had strayed from some Italian square. It is a shame that no use could be found for it when its pumping days were over. While these, and other buildings were built in Victorian Worksop, one with a history that spanned the centuries, all but disappeared.

This was Worksop Manor. Virtually rebuilt in palatial style after it was damaged by fire in 1761, it was acquired by the Duke of Newcastle in 1840. Already owning Clumber House and not needing another home so close to it, he ordered its demolition. As its walls began to fall, Mrs. Emma Wilmott, the wife of the Duke's agent and a talented artist, recorded the last days of the once famous house. Happily that was not the end of its story for the surviving domestic quarters were converted to the smaller though quite substantial Manor that stands today.

Much more could be written about 19th century Worksop and, indeed, has been.[22] Sufficient to add that although it was a time of change it was but a foretaste of what was to happen in the years that followed. Its population continued to grow and by the year 2000 it had reached around 36,000, the houses necessary to accommodate the increase pushing out into the surrounding countryside. Since 1974 Worksop had formed part of the administrative district of Bassetlaw which also includes Retford and the whole of North Nottinghamshire formerly the responsibility of the Worksop and Retford Rural District Councils. As Worksop had only enjoyed borough status since 1931 it seemed, to some, a shame to lose it so quickly and no longer to have the presence of its own mayor at civic and town occasions. Those today, who as children in 1931 recall the procession and market place ceremony that celebrated the award of Worksop's borough charter will have lived through the many changes that have taken place in the town. Some of these have been beneficial: others have brought problems that have yet to be solved. Those affecting industry and employment have been the most far reaching. For centuries, the town's work pattern was based on the soil; farming, milling, malting and timber working. Of these, malting has disappeared and the other three provide the livelihood for a mere handful. Mining, which dominated the industrial scene for close on one hundred and fifty years is now but a memory. In their place a number of new industries have been introduced but they have only partially taken up the slack in unemployment and many local people are without regular work.

Sixty or so years ago most of the town's work force either walked or cycled to mine, factory, office or shop. No school catering for older children was complete without its bicycle shed and many shops used them to deliver their goods. Their virtual replacement by motor vehicles and their continuing increase in numbers has created a traffic problem in Worksop that it shares with most other towns in the country. Pedestrianisation, one way streets, on street parking restrictions and a by pass have been introduced but the problem of fitting twenty first century traffic into a nineteenth century road system is one that remains and baffles solution. As the roads become more congested, two other ways of transport have enjoyed something of a revival. On the 7th January, 2000 two boats sailed along the Chesterfield Canal from Worksop to Shireoaks, the first to make the passage for fifty years. This was a trial run and marked the culmination of several years of restoration work. By the summer this stretch of the waterway was fully open and boats were able to moor in a marina which has been converted from the basin where the working boats of bygone days used to be loaded with coal from the nearby colliery. Meanwhile work on the canal beyond Shireoaks continued and, before long, boats were able to sail to Turner Wood and even to Kiveton. It is envisaged that the restored waterway will be essentially a leisure amenity. While an occasional specialised cargo may be carried, the day of the working boat is over.

Not so on the railway where the re-opening of the line to Nottingham in 1998 inaugurated an hourly service between Worksop and the county town. This improvement must be weighed against the almost total withdrawal of passenger trains from what originally was the main line to the east coast. Now only three trains a week, all on a Saturday, run between Worksop and Cleethorpes. Once the hub of so much activity, between trains the station looks virtually deserted. There is no longer any platform bustle or, indeed, any platform staff and passenger facilities are minimal. However, unlike Gainsborough, Brigg and several smaller places along the line, the station still stands and has recently been cleaned and renovated, and once again boasts refreshment facilities.

Bus passengers are less well catered for. For many years, from the 1930's until the 1950's buses set out for their various destinations from Hardy Street, Ryton Street and Queen Street. The situation then improved when a covered bus station was opened. It was rather cramped, the air was heavy with diesel fumes but, at least, it provided shelter from the rain. Even this was soon to be denied to local bus users. Needing greater garage space, the station was closed in 1977, would be passengers having to await their services on the pavement of Hardy Street. Better is in prospect as a new bus station has been promised for the early years of the 21st. century.

In contrast with earlier years, church and chapel going decreased. For the Anglicans, the three parish churches of the Priory, St. John's and St. Annes have their loyal supporters though they are fewer than in the past. Structurally, the Priory was enhanced, in the eyes of some, by the addition of a stumpy central tower, a needle-like spire and the re-building of its east end. A new church at Manton, dedicated in 1968 provided a brief sign of growth and the Roman Catholics felt strong enough to build a second church, St. Joseph's, which stands amid the new houses of the Prospect estate to the north of the town. It is in the non-conformist churches where the decline is most apparent. At the beginning of the century their chapels were well supported and their influence in the town was strong in local government, business activities and trade unionism. Mayor's Sunday often meant a long trudge for the band, town council and various organisations to a service at the Primitive Methodist chapel at the top of John Street. The days of such prominence have long passed, dwindling to two chapels that are gradually moving towards union and occasional services at a mission chapel. Making up, in part, for this loss are a number of Pentecostal churches where, to their members, the form of worship seems more appropriate to the present time. These have developed during the later decades of the century. One that has been present throughout is the Salvation Army. On the streets and at their Citadel, their witness has been constant. Little more need be said about 20th century Worksop. At its end it spreads over a far greater area, in general living conditions are much improved, its population is much more varied in origin and its economic future less certain.

To many eyes the town is less attractive than it was and it is a shame that the present more stringent planning controls and more enlightened views on conservation were not in being much earlier. All to often ugliness has replaced elegance to the detriment of the appearance of the main streets. Timber framed buildings of Tudor times, graceful Georgian houses, even the decorated facade of a Victorian public hall, later the town's first cinema, all have gone. This is unfortunate but would not have been so sad had they been replaced by buildings of quality. In many instances this was not so. All too often they have been succeeded by featureless, box-like structures of materials that clash rather than harmonise with their neighbours.

No century has brought about more changes in Worksop than the twentieth. People returning to the town after a long absence would be hard pressed to recognise where they were. Much, though not quite all, of the town is encircled by a bypass and while the road layout within is not much changed, the types of shops along its streets have changed radically. Out of town supermarkets have drawn custom from the centre, the multiple has almost driven out the locally owned shop, the provision market is declining and the cattle market has been long closed. In the evening the change is just as marked. Gone are the four cinemas that drew people into the town centre in their hundreds. One, however, the Regal, has survived as an Arts Centre and does show films, albeit in a much smaller auditorium than in the past. Its future seems much in the balance while talk of a multi-screen cinema, at the time of writing, is no more than speculation. Similarly lost to the town are the two dance halls, each with its resident band, though one of them, the former Palais de Danse still stands as a venue for Bingo. Lest this seems a list of vanished pleasures, today a leisure centre and several gymnasia cater for those in quest of fitness, disco music pounds away until the early hours in a number of night clubs, cricket, football, hockey and rugby teams provide sporting entertainment while a host of clubs and societies offer opportunities for people of like interests to meet together. Correspondence and comments in the local paper often voice dis-satisfaction with the town and its amenities but this, probably, has always been so. What is to be hoped, as the town moves forward into the 21st. century, is that, while taking advantage of appropriate developments in building method and technology, it will also strive to retain its own character and heritage. In the hope that this will be so, these words are set down as the writer's personal contribution to that end.

Notes and References

1. Scratta Wood lies between Shireoaks and Steetley.

2. J.E.B. Gover, Allan Mawer, F.M. Stenton. The Place Names of Nottinghamshire

3. The late Mr. Eliot G. Warburton, a Worksop solicitor, collected fifty eight different spellings of Worksop.

4. The object dates from the middle 9th century and is of the Trewhiddle type. It is now in the Bassetlaw Museum.

5. He is sometimes referred to as Roger de Busli.

6. John Leland.

7. This is a mis-nomer. The monastery at Worksop was a priory, not an abbey, hence the street and the three abbey schools were wrongly named. The Revd. H.J. Slodden, Vicar of Worksop, tried to correct this in 1887 though with little success.

8. The number varied. There were 19 at the foundation, 16 at the dissolution.

9. Sanctity and Scandal. Published by The Continuing Education Press of the University of Nottingham, 1993.

10. John Fox. The Tickhill Psalter. The Nottinghamshire Historian, Autumn 2000 and Winter 2001.

11. W. Shakespeare. King Henry VI Part 1. Act 4, Scene 7.

12. Hugh Talbot. The English Achilles. 1961.

13. A.C. Wood. A Note on the Population of Six Notts. Towns in the 17th Century. The Transactions of the Thoroton Society, Vol. 41. 1937.

14. Ibid.

15. G. Scurfield. Early 17th Century Worksop and its Environs. The Transactions of the Thoroton Society, Vol. 90. 1986.

16. Ibid.

17. Quarter Sessions Minute Book, 1655.

18. Vicar of Worksop, 1601 - 1613.

19. S.D. Chapman in "The Pioneers of Worsted Spinning by Power" suggests that both were close to the canal.

20. The Dictionary of National Biography

21. These matters are treated in greater detail in the author's book "Victorian Worksop"

22. Ibid.

An Old Lady Looks Back.

Mrs. Hannah Beeston lived the greater part of her life in a small cottage down a narrow courtyard that ran back from Gateford Road.   The scene shown on this photograph would be familiar to her as an old lady though she would remember some of the shops and houses being built as many of them date to the 19th century.   The opening of Shireoaks colliery in 1859 gave a boost to the development of the whole area.

Hannah Hodgkinson was born in the early years of the 19th century and was still alive at the dawn of the 20th. In the summer of 1901 she spoke to a reporter from the recently founded Worksop Guardian[1] and the interview was recorded in a subsequent edition of the paper.[2] Then in her 95th year, she was a little deaf but otherwise in full possession of her faculties. In particular, memories of her early childhood years were especially vivid.

She was born on the 28th April, 1807 and baptised at the Priory Church just under a month later on the 24th May. Her parents were named as Joseph and Sarah Hodgkinson. Unusual for the time, Hannah received a little formal education. She attended what she called the Free School on Newgate Street. This was maintained by the church, the equivalent school for boys being held in the Priory Gatehouse. Many years after Hannah had left, the school moved, in 1840, to new premises close to the church and was thereafter known as the Abbey Girls' School. Her time at Newgate Street was brief and her scholastic achievements meagre. She learned to read but, apparently, failed to master writing as at her wedding, was only able to make her mark in the register. A family tragedy brought to an end her time in class. When she was eleven, her mother died and Hannah, as best she could, had to look after the family home.

No doubt she was already familiar with the round of chores that was the housewife's lot at that time and would soon find that the daily routine of cleaning, washing, cooking and shopping left her little free time. Whatever spare moments she did have, however, she put to good use. "Girls had more to do in those days than they have now," she reminisced to the Guardian reporter. Housework done, young Hannah took out her spinning wheel and earned a few coppers by producing thread for some weavers who lived in Norfolk Street. These were the last days of such home manufacture in Worksop

Old names die hard. Although this part of Worksop was called Victoria Square in 1887 in honour of Queen Victoria's Golden Jubilee, its old, unofficial, name of the Common End persisted for many years. Mrs. Beeston made her way from her home to Pennington's shop on the corner with Carlton Road, to collect her old age pension and to buy her weekly copy of the Worksop Guardian.

and it would be interesting to know how many more spinning wheels and, indeed, weaving looms were in active use in the town. In days gone by sufficient cloth was produced to justify part of Lead Hill being used as a tenter green, a place where lengths of material were stretched out to dry.[3] It had long ceased to be used for such a purpose when Hannah delivered her thread to the weavers. The cloth that they wove was hard wearing and some of it was made up into shirts by industrious wives and daughters. No doubt this was yet another of Hannah's tasks. Just a little critically, she mused on the way times had changed since her girlhood. "Some folks nowadays would sooner buy a ready made shirt that goes to pieces very soon, than be at the trouble of making one."

Hannah Hodgkinson married quite young on the 5th September, 1826. She was nineteen. Her husband was George Beeston and he was five years older than his bride. The ceremony took place at the Priory Church and was performed by the vicar, the Revd. Thomas Stacye. Then quite elderly, rather absent minded and suffering from a speech defect, he was banned from the pulpit in 1832 though he clung on to his living until his death in 1847.[4] At different times George Beeston was described as a boatman, landlord of the Anchor Inn and a labourer in a woodyard. Whatever his occupation, his wage packet was never large. Life for the Beestons was far from easy, though doubtless, Hannah's early experience in housekeeping made every shilling go as far as it possibly could. Their home was down one of the courts that then ran from Gateford Road. Small, hemmed in and lacking in amenity as it was, it would take all of Mrs. Beeston's determination and ingenuity to keep it clean and make it comfortable. From what can be judged of her character she would surely accomplish this. Children's laughter never brightened the little cottage as the Beestons had no family, though rather than let the second bedroom remain empty, they took in a succession of lodgers, a bricklayer in 1861, two joiners ten years later and Mrs. Beeston's nephew, a miner and his wife in 1891.

Not all Mrs. Beeston's recollections were of the hard grind of everyday existence: occasional high days stood out more vividly. One such was when Queen Victoria passed through the town. That was on the 18th September 1835 when the princess was returning from a visit to Earl Fitzwilliam at Wentworth Woodhouse. Presumably she entered the town along Gateford Road so Mrs. Beeston would only have to walk a few yards to the end of her court to see her. What she thought of this glimpse of the heir to the throne is not known, though Mr. Dawson, the proprietor of the Lion, where the royal carriage paused to change horses, felt that it was too modest an equipage for so important a person. He insisted on providing four horses with postillions, and driving himself as far as the next staging post at the Hop Pole at Ollerton. Princess Victoria, so the town gossips had it, was most impressed.[5]

Although Mrs. Beeston lived all her life

This photograph shows a yard off Gateford Road, no doubt very similar to the one where Mrs. Beeston lived. The cottages that were packed into these yards were often badly built, of cramped accommodation and lacking in basic facilities.

in Worksop, she did venture out of the town from time to time. She recalled travelling by the "Tally Ho" coach up into Yorkshire and, on a later occasion, going by train to London. This may have been quicker than by road but it certainly wasn't any more comfortable. She rode in an open truck, at the mercy of the weather and begrimed by smoke and smuts from the engine. On another journey her sister was badly burned on the neck by a flying spark. Later in her life, Mrs.Beeston would see an ever increasing number of bicycles on the town's streets and may, had she been up and about early enough on the 11th May, 1900, have seen a procession of motor cars drive down Gateford Road and into town. There were over fifty of them and they were taking part in a thousand mile trial organized by the Automobile Association.

It was however, in the past that Mrs. Beeston mainly dwelt. She spoke of races held on Gateford Road when girls and boys ran for lengths of home spun cloth, of walking "up t'street" to the market before the Town Hall was built when the stalls were set up round the ramshackle Moot Hall near the Old Ship, those selling pots straggling down Potter Street, as they had from time immemorial.

As with so many of her fellow townspeople, life had always been hard for Mrs. Beeston but she had risen to its challenge and had won through. Great sadness there had been as when her husband died as long ago as May, 1870 but it was memories of happier days that filled her mind. In her 95th year she was living on her own, able to do a little housework, washing and cooking and looking forward to the arrival each evening of a niece who spent the night with her. She could still manage to walk into town and a few days before her interview she had been as far as the office of the Worksop Gas Company to pay her bill. Not as far as that but every Friday she made her way to Pennington's on Victoria Square to buy her copy of the Worksop Guardian which she read avidly. As she sat down to peruse the issue of the 23rd. August, 1901, she would doubtless smile as the account of her interview brought back even more memories of her long life throughout almost the whole of the nineteenth century.

Notes and References

1. The first issue of the Worksop Guardian appeared on the 27th March, 1896.
2. The Worksop Guardian, 23rd August, 1901.
3. The term was used in John Harrison's Survey of the Manor of Worksop of 1636. By 1841 just five weavers were still at work.
4. M.J.Jackson, Victorian Worksop, pages 71 and 74.
5. The Worksop Guardian, 14th May, 1909.

A Man of his Time.

Hard in business yet generous in charity: a pillar of the church: active in local government: a man of property and influence: such a description might be applied to the traditional Victorian who had prospered in life. It certainly fitted Joseph Garside who, for over forty years, was a dominant personality in Worksop. Today one short street recalls his name: one hundred years ago there was not one street where his name was not known.

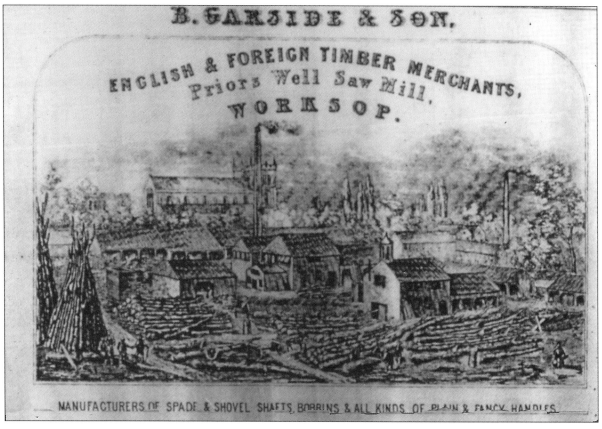

Joseph Garside's timber yard occupied much of the land to the east of Priorswell Road, stretching from the canal to the Priory Church. Until the development of Shireoaks and Steetley collieries, he was the largest employer in Worksop. This engraving formed the letterhead of the firm's stationery.

Joseph Garside was born in 1820. His father, Benjamin Garside, a young man in his early twenties was setting up as a timber merchant with his yard off Priorswell Road. It was not until 1832 that his business was mentioned in a local directory.[1] Then, in partnership with another Joseph, presumably his brother, he was described as an English timber dealer, sawyer and hedge carpenter.

Little is known of young Joseph's education though, at best, it was likely to have been short and his accomplishments limited. The tradition that he was illiterate is probably an exaggeration. He could certainly write his name as his signature has survived on a number of documents. Like many of his contemporaries he was soon at work, joining his father in the timber yard. Within a few years the firm gained a contract that was to set it on the road to expansion and greater prosperity. This was to supply timber for the proposed North Midland Railway which was to link Derby with Leeds and pass within ten miles of Worksop between Renishaw and Eckington. Shortly after its completion, though still in his early twenties, Joseph Garside was taken into partnership with his father. The two men worked hard, the firm did well and, in 1858, the year of Benjamin's death - he was 61 - it was the biggest timber business in the town, its yard stretching southwards from the canal towards the Priory Church.

Joseph Garside served on the Worksop Local Board of Health for almost twenty years, for much of that time as its chairman. Under his leadership, the Board undertook the draining and sewage disposal of the town, the culmination of which was the opening of the pumping station off Bracebridge on the 19th August, 1881. Although Garside had retired from the Board by then, much of the success of the scheme was due to his determination and single-mindedness.

By 1861, on the threshold of his forties, Joseph Garside appeared to be gathering in the rewards of his industry. With his two teenage daughters he lived at Carlton House where a cook, a housemaid and a kitchen maid took the rough edges off the domestic work. At his timber yard he employed one hundred and forty two men and twelve boys. Additionally he owned a farm of over one hundred acres [2] and in the town was starting to buy up land and property when it came on the market. Home and work apart, he was also beginning to cut a dash in civic affairs, being chairman of the Local Board of Health. Such success and outward prosperity had not been achieved without times of sadness and inward grief. Missing from the many rooms and spacious grounds of Carlton House was his second wife Catherine and his youngest child of the same name. Both had died during the previous decade.

At about this time Joseph Garside began to expand his business interests. With fellow townsman Daniel Fossick Alderson as partner he founded the Priorwell Brewery Company. Using the water from the well traditionally linked with Worksop Priory and supposedly the cause of miraculous cures in bygone days it is not surprising that the brewery did well. A seeming set back in 1861 when Mr. Alderson died while duck shooting at

Clumber was turned to advantage as it led to the amalgamation with Worksop's other brewery, that of Smith and Nephew at Creswell Holme. The new firm, the Worksop and Retford Brewery Company, appointed Joseph Garside as its chairman and William Allen, of Smith and Nephew, as its managing director. Soon all brewing was carried out at the Priorswell Road premises and so Garside's two main business interests were but a hundred or so yards apart, a few minutes walk. This was an undoubted convenience to him as he took an interest in all that transpired: "no detail was too small for his attention."[3] Also in the town, he was a substantial shareholder in the Worksop Gas Light and Coke Company though he took no part in its management

Outside Worksop, Joseph Garside was associated with a number of firms, chiefly around Sheffield. He was chairman and managing director of Wells Brothers of Renishaw and had interests in Brown, Bailey of Sheffield, Davy Brothers of Sheffield, Garside and Shaw, timber merchants of Sheffield and the Tinsley Iron Works and Collieries. And that was not all. Rather surprisingly for one living so far inland, he had a number of maritime interests. He was concerned with a boat building business at Burton-upon-Stather, on the River Trent, was a shareholder in a shipbuilding company at Goole and had connections with a fishing fleet at Grimsby. Not all his business ventures prospered though most of them did, so much so that the local paper could comment, "His success on the other hand in nearly all he undertook was remarkable".[4]

Under the Public Health Act of 1848 a General Board of Health was established and one of its prime responsibilities was to authorise the setting up of Local Boards of Health in urban areas. Such boards were essentially local councils and were mainly concerned with drainage, sewage disposal, highway maintenance, water supply and such matters. In 1852 Worksop voted for its first Local Board of Health. Joseph Garside stood as a candidate but was unsuccessful and it was not until 1856 that he was elected a member. Making up for this delay, his promotion was swift, for in the following year he became its chairman, holding the position until he resigned in 1875.

A lasting memorial to his work on the Board was the town's drainage system. Prior to this the disposal of

Little happened in the second half of the 19th century in Worksop that did not involve Joseph Garside. When a committee was formed to consider the building of a new church, he was immediately made a member. Its deliberations led to the creation of St. John's Church in 1869. Joseph Garside's contribution was not confined to advice at meetings. He also provided the land upon which the church was built and donated £1,000 to the building fund.

household waste had been, at best, haphazard, at worst non-existent. Although the town boasted of the purity of its air, this claim would have been disproved by a walk on a warm summer's day among the more crowded, poorer parts and visitations of cholera, typhus and typhoid were not unknown. The main drainage of the town was begun in 1859 under the supervision of Robert Rawlinson. His scheme caused widespread interest but was not fully successful. Almost twenty years elapsed before an attempt was made to improve matters. Then the work was entrusted to the Local Board's own surveyor, John Allsopp. Under the system that he devised the treated waste was pumped onto the fields of Kilton Forest Farm. The culmination of many years of work and concern came on the 19th August, 1881 when a new pumping station on Bracebridge was officially set in operation. By then Joseph Garside was no longer a member of the Local Board though much of the preliminary work had been carried out under his chairmanship and the bulk of the £37,000 borrowed for town improvements during that time had been spent on its implementation.

That Joseph Garside was a valued and conscientious member of the Local Board cannot be doubted neither that his sympathies were for the well being of the townspeople. These considerations make his attitude to the provision of piped water seem rather puzzling. It was obvious to many that this was necessary. Worksop's drinking water came from pump, well, rainwater butt and even the canal and much of it, especially in the crowded parts of the town was contaminated. The inadequacy of supply and the poor quality of the water was both the bane of the inhabitants and the concern of visiting government inspectors, one of whom wrote, "The water supply and drainage are of the most wretched description, and manure heaps, piggeries, foul privies and stagnant filth flourish in the vicinity of the houses. The accumulated filth percolates to the wells and pollutes the water which people drink."[5]

Piped water was clearly one solution to this unsatisfactory situation. Some prominent townsmen began agitating for this but Joseph Garside was adamantly opposed to it. Before the Local Board and at public meetings he stated his reasons. Sufficient good water was available for everyone, he said, and it was the responsibility of property owners to ensure that it was accessible to their tenants. "I am a large owner of property, and I would not allow any of my tenants to suffer in health for want of good water," were his words on the 11th March, 1875 at a public meeting at the Town Hall [6] He felt that a private waterworks company was not necessary, it would not be financially viable and could, in the future, lead the Board to considerable expense should it have to bail out a failing company. Additionally, he felt that the Board had sufficient on its hands with the seemingly never ending saga of the drainage scheme. His eloquence carried the meeting and it was agreed to oppose the implementation of the waterworks bill. This did not daunt its supporters and they demanded a poll of the ratepayers of the parish. Flushed with temporary success, Mr. Garside said that this, "would be granted cheerfully." He was not so cheerful at the outcome, for the poll reversed the decision of the meeting and registered a two to one majority in favour of the waterworks scheme.

Joseph Garside's reaction was immediate. He resigned from the Local Board both as its chairman and as a member.

Whatever gloom may have pervaded the council chamber at his resignation, it is likely that there was a far happier atmosphere in Garside's home for a new family was growing up at Carlton House. In the late 1860's he had married Mary Shelton Eddison of Shireoaks. She bore him six children, sons Abraham and Frederick and a daughter Isilene, the other three dying in infancy. Striking a pleasant domestic note in later years, when recalling her father to her own daughter, Isilene always spoke of him with great affection.[7]

Not that his resignation added greatly to the time he spent at home: his diary was always well filled. Even while still on the Local Board he was also a hard working member of the building committee of St. John's Church. This interest lasted for ten years, beginning at a public meeting held on the 22nd. May, 1862 and ending on the 14th September, 1872 when the church had already been in use for three years. During that time he attended fifty-eight committee meetings as well as serving on sub-committees and deputations. Garside's contribution to the building was not confined to time and counsel. He gave £1,000 to the building fund and also sold one of his many pieces of land, known as the Tanyard, for its site. There is no doubt that his energy; his business experience and his status in the town were significant features in the satisfactory building of the church. Well could its historian write at a much later date, "It is fair to say that the quality and stability of St.John's Church as it stands today after 100 years is largely owing to the watchful care of Joseph Garside in conjunction with the Clerk of Works, Henry Spooner".[8]

Plans for the medical as well as the spiritual well being of his fellow townspeople also received Garside's support. Prior to 1867 those who were ill or had suffered injury were dependent on local doctors or the infirmary of the Union Workhouse for treatment. The former expected payment for their services and the latter was only resorted to as a desperate measure. In that year Viscountess Galway of Serlby, with money that she had collected, bought a house on Potter Street and opened it as a dispensary. For a trial period of two years she personally supervised its working with a committee to help her. After that time she vested its oversight in three trustees: Joseph Garside was one of them. In addition to this administrative help he also subscribed ten guineas a year towards its running costs, an amount only exceeded by the Duke and Duchess of Newcastle.

He put his hand even deeper into his pocket in support of the Nurse's Home. In 1871 Lady Gertrude Foljambe of Osberton had arranged and paid for a nurse to live and work in the town. Joseph Garside fully approved of this but thought that her services would be more effective if she had her own home in the centre of the town where everyone would know where to find her. On hearing of his idea, Mrs. Emily Linley of Netherholme gave a plot of land on the opposite side of Bridge Place to her house as a site for the home. It was built largely at Garside's expense and subscriptions were invited to support the work of the nurse. Despite the generosity of a number of people there was never sufficient to cover the envisaged expenses of £100 a year.

So matters stood at the beginning of 1887 when much local interest centred on how the town might best mark Queen Victoria's forthcoming Golden Jubilee. To discuss the matter formally a public meeting was held on the 27th January in the Town Hall. After the chairman's opening remarks, Mr. Garside stood up and spoke about the Nurse's Home, detailing its history and proposing that it would be a fitting act for Jubilee year to raise a sufficient fund so that the work of the home could be adequately endowed. He estimated that £2,800 would be necessary for this and offered, there and then, to start the collection with a donation of £1,000. The Rt. Hon. F.J.S. Foljambe of Osberton seconded the proposal and promised £150 to supplement Garside's gift. Faced with such generosity the meeting could do nothing but agree. There were a few other suggestions and comments but they came to nothing. Garside could back his scheme with cash and so he had his way. No one questioned his motives: all applauded his munificence but a lot neither liked his idea nor the way by which he had attained its fulfilment. This was apparent when the collecting boxes were out. The appeal was disappointingly supported. By the 20th May less than £1,700 had been received, well below the target figure. Never the less, the home was endowed and its occupant served the town well.

Joseph Garside emerges as a man who never did things by halves: his commitment to any cause or interest that he embraced was total. So it was with politics. He was a staunch and unwavering Liberal throughout his life: a prominent figure in the political life of Bassetlaw. He was largely responsible for securing Mr. Fox Bristowe as a last minute candidate for the ill-fated by-election of 1876 and was deeply grieved when the polling day demonstrations and disturbances were attributed to Liberal agitation.[9] One of the happier aspects of his political work was his long friendship and association with the Rt. Hon. F.J.S. Foljambe but this too suffered its set backs. In 1886 the two men found themselves on opposite sides in the schism that split the Liberal party asunder following the introduction of Mr. Gladstone's Irish Home Rule Bill. Garside remained faithful to Mr. Gladstone while Mr. Foljambe followed those who opposed their leader's attempt to reduce the troubles in Ireland. Also in 1886 Mr. Garside helped to found the Worksop Liberal Association and let them use the rooms of the Criterion Hall which he had bought three years earlier. Perhaps, at their meetings, discussing future plans and hopes with like-minded friends, he gained some consolation for the political disappointments and frustrations of the past.

Following Garside's resignation from the Local Board of Health in 1875 there were attempts to make him consider re-election. These he declined. Having once made up his mind, he refused to change it. However, when another way opened of serving in local government he took advantage of it and, in 1888, he was one of the first members elected to the newly formed Nottinghamshire County Council.

During the summer of 1893, in his seventy third year, while still a county councillor, still a trustee of the Worksop Savings Bank, still a member of the Board of Guardians, still a trustee of the dispensary, still working for the Nurse's Home and still immersed in business matters, Joseph Garside developed bronchitis. For some years his once robust health had been deteriorating and a "complication of disorders"[10] had caused him to be more careful. With his wife and family he went to Buxton where his condition worsened and after six days, on Sunday the 16th July, he died. News of his death reached Worksop by telegram early on Monday morning. The town was stunned. People refused to accept the news until it was confirmed. The man who for over forty years had been the dominant personality in the town, whose generosity and benevolence were unrivalled, who owned much property and land in the town was dead. Perhaps those were right, who, on that melancholy Monday, nodded their heads and said that his like would never be seen again. The funeral was held on Wednesday and on the following Sunday references to his life and work were made from every pulpit in the town, both in church and chapel. As an additional tribute the Worksop Brass Band, at its Sunday afternoon concert on the cricket ground, played the Dead March.

When a man involved himself so fully in the life of the town, as Joseph Garside did, it is comparatively easy to find out about his activities and interests. Some of these have been mentioned. What is more difficult is to discover the sort of man he was. Such qualities as industriousness, tirelessness and generosity immediately come to mind though it would be reasonable to suggest that he was also a man who liked his own way and could be rather over-bearing, even a little pig-headed at times. Whatever his feelings, though, reports in the local paper indicate that he always remained courteous and equable in public debate and at meetings. A surviving portrait [11] reveals the face of such a man: strong, determined, intelligent: a youngish face, clean shaven apart from long side whiskers. It was a no nonsense face: perhaps not one that could easily break into a laugh but, let it be hoped, one that could evince a look of satisfaction at the end of a hard day's work well done. It may be fanciful but not unfitting to leave so active and vigorous a man as Joseph Garside in a rare moment of relaxation in the conservatory of his home at Carlton House. There, "where the hyacinth, narcissi, lily of the valley and the tea roses fill the air with their fresh and varied perfumes,"[12] he could pause awhile and refresh himself, ready for all the demands that the next day might bring.

During Garside's life there was much speculation in the town on the extent of his wealth. The publication of his will revealed that he left upwards of £166,000 [13] a sum undreamt of by most of his contemporaries and a fitting achievement for his business ability, his tireless energy and his relentless ambition.

Notes and References

1. Whites Directory of Nottinghamshire 1832

2. Census Returns, 1861

3. The Retford and Gainsborough Times 1893

4. Ibid

5. Government Inspectors Report, 1853

6. The Retford and Gainsborough Times March, 13th. 1875

7. I was told this by Mrs.Smith of Carlton.

8. W.Straw. St. John's Church Worksop.1869-1969

9. See "A Worksop Diary", pages, 97,98 for further details.

10. The Retford and Gainsborough Times July 1st. 1893.

11. W.Straw. St. John's Church Worksop.1869-1969 opposite page 15

12. The Retford and Gainsborough Times March, 25th. 1881

13. Ibid. October, 6th. 1893

PICTURE SUPPLEMENT, 1
HENRY HODGES: MAN OF MANY PARTS.

Henry Hodges was a man of various talents. By trade he was a grocer and his shop still stands on the corner of Eastgate with George Street. As a young man he was a member of the Sherwood Rangers Yeomanry, was one of the best shots in the regiment and rose to the rank of Quartermaster Sergeant. In civic affairs, for over twenty years he was secretary of the Worksop Traders' Association and a founder of the Plate -Glass Society.

It was, however, as a musician that he was widest known and this rare photograph shows him at the harmonium of the chapel of the Union Workhouse on Eastgate. In these bleak surroundings he played at services for over fifty years, and he also served as organist and choirmaster at different times, at both St. John's Church and the Congregational Chapel. Mr. Hodges died on the 27th February 1927 at the age of 72.

A Long Forgotten Chapel.

Browsers at book fairs, while perhaps, from time to time, finding an acceptable addition to their collections, will only rarely light upon something that is so totally unexpected that its acquisition becomes an absolute necessity. Such an experience was that of the writer at a recent fair at Buxton. There, somewhat solitary among the thousands of books, lying on a table, was a water colour painting of a building that had a vaguely familiar look to it. A glance at the inscription confirmed the identification. It read, "Independent Chapel, Worksop, 1865.

When, in 1865, an unknown artist, painted this picture of the Independent (later Congregational) Chapel on Westgate, it was going through difficult times. Low in membership and short of funds, imminent closure was contemplated. However the members decided against this and resolved to build a new chapel. This proved a long process and it was not until 1876 that their new premises on Bridge Place were ready for occupation.

Any picture of that period of a North Nottinghamshire subject immediately raises the question whether it was painted by James Walsham Baldock. Though born at Tadcaster, he spent the greater part of his life at Worksop. From the late 1840's until 1884, when he moved to Nottingham, he painted many local landscapes and portraits as well as the animal studies and hunting scenes upon which his reputation is now mainly based. Not long ago a few pounds would have bought one of his pictures, now they are much more highly prized and it is perhaps natural to wish to attribute any likely painting to his brush. Unfortunately, the most careful scrutiny has failed to reveal either signature or monogram on this picture. The artist remains just as anonymous as are the people he depicted making their way to Sunday service.

That there were only a few of them was quite usual as the church was but moderately supported throughout its somewhat chequered history. A first attempt to establish an Independent church in Worksop was made in 1807 when some students from the denominational college at Rotherham held a few services in the town. Attendance was not encouraging and the project was soon discontinued. Perhaps the choice of venue did not help. Although used at different times by other non-conformist churches, it was in a poor part of the town where many would not choose to tread. Standing on Bedlam Square, situated above a stable and next to a slaughter house, the room was used during the week as a school. In 1824 the Independents once more tried to gain a footing in the town this time meeting at the house of a Mr. Gilling that stood on the corner of Potter Street with Priorswell Road. Attendance clearly exceeded accommodation and after two Sundays the premises in the inauspiciously named Bedlam Square were again hired. For five years services were led by student ministers from Rotherham College until, in 1829, the congregation felt sufficiently strong, both numerically and financially, to call its own minister. He was the Revd. William Joseph and it was under his leadership and guidance that the infant church aspired to build its own place of worship. Work began in 1830 and by mid 1831 the building depicted on the painting was complete and in use. It did, however, differ in one detail from the picture. There the date stone above the door showed the year 1838 whereas it should have read 1830. Perhaps the artist's skill was better than his memory.

One piece of good fortune had helped the Worksop Independents in their chapel building. The Duke of Norfolk, owner of Worksop Manor and much property in the town, though a Roman Catholic by faith, generously allowed them a site at a nominal rent. The first that was chosen proved unsuitable and it was exchanged for the one on Westgate where the chapel was built. As was usual at that time, it was almost square in plan, measuring thirteen yards across the front and fifteen in depth. Built of stone, it had an unpretentious though dignified appearance. Entrance was by a central door that was flanked by a large round-headed window on either side. Above the door was the date stone and, just discernable on the painting, a small, rectangular window. Two large windows in each side wall helped to flood the interior with light on a summer's day. The building was set back a little from the road and separated from it by a low wall topped with iron railings. Part of the grounds was used for burials, the rest planted with shrubs and young trees. By the time of the picture, three of these had matured and grown to roof height. The word "neat" was often used to describe early non-conformist meeting houses. It certainly applied to that of the Independents of Worksop.

For a small group of people, none of whom were of more than modest means, its completion was a remarkable achievement. Not only did they strain their own pockets and purses to cover the building costs but they also sought help from far and wide. A note book, containing an appeal from Mr. Joseph on its first page, was circulated to both individuals and churches over an extensive area. Those wishing to make donations were asked to enter details before returning the book. Perhaps some of the money so obtained helped to pay for the raised and centrally situated pulpit, the focal point for all the eyes of the congregation. It cost £14 - 10 - 0d. (£14.50), the most expensive piece of furniture in the chapel. Each of the thirteen long pews cost £3 and the sixteen short ones £1 - 10 - 0d. (£1.50). Should they all have been fully occupied, they would have seated two hundred and seventy five people but this was rarely, if ever, so. When it was opened on the 2nd. June, 1831 just eighteen people, eleven women and seven men, formally signed a covenant that constituted them as a church. Though numbers did increase, growth was but slow. The Independents were very careful in admitting new members and those wishing to join had first to be proposed, then visited in their homes and finally approved at a church meeting. These hurdles having been surmounted, members were expected to be regular in attendance, seemly in behaviour and to participate fully in church meetings at which decisions in all matters, both spiritual and administrative, were taken. Those failing to live up to these expectations were either suspended or expelled from membership. In 1833 an anonymous backslider, "having been found guilty of misconduct," was suspended for twelve months. More serious was the case of William Chapell in 1837. He was expelled for drunkenness "and other irregularities" while his wife was suspended, "for non-attendance and other unchristian conduct." Apparently John and Ann Battersby were involved in the same affair and,

The chapel suffered a major setback in 1848 when its second minister, the Revd. William Hugill resigned. He continued to live in Worksop and attracted a number of his former congregation to services which he first held in his home and, later, in the building shown on this picture. Standing on Lead Hill, it was known as Hugill's Chapel.

"the church after calm investigation unanimously exculpated the former though did not regard the latter as free from censure."

However, such meagre evidence as has survived suggests that Mr. Joseph's ministry was acceptable and, in the main, harmonious and that his resignation on the 6th October, 1839 was received with genuine regret. His farewell sermon was preached, so it was recorded, "to an overflowing congregation." The calling of a minister in the Independent Church was rarely a speedy matter and seventeen months elapsed before a successor to Mr. Joseph was appointed. He was the Revd. William Hugill and he began his pastorate on the 21st. March, 1841. During the interregnum students from the college at Rotherham had helped with services.

After the Congregationalists moved to Bridge Place in 1876, their former chapel was converted to living accommodation. Later it was used as a store. When this photograph was taken in 1966 it had been long abandoned. It was finally demolished in 1972.

Mr. Hugill proved a zealous minister, a man of deep spirituality and a stickler for correctness in all church matters. He was clearly unhappy about the way in which the church had been established in 1831 and, on his suggestion, it was re-modelled. As a result of this, twenty seven people re-affirmed their membership. An increase of only nine over a decade on the number of founding members may seem but tardy growth as, on the face of it, it was but it should not be regarded as a true indication of support. Attendance almost invariably exceeded membership in 19th century non-conformist places of worship and that was certainly so at Worksop. Of the twenty seven who constituted "this Christian church" in 1841, all save three were women though it would be unrealistic to suppose that they formed so marked a majority of the congregation. At this time fewer men chose to commit themselves to full membership though some of them were not averse to helping in other ways. In 1841 six of them were appointed to form a managing committee, "to superintend the temporal concerns of the chapel."

Within six months of Mr. Hugill's arrival an extension had been built onto the back of the chapel to provide separate accommodation for the Sunday School. This is shown on the painting of 1865 and, if the artist's use of colour was correct, it was of brick. That there was need for it was obvious as there were already eighty children on the roll of the Sunday School, meeting, it would seem, in odd corners of the chapel. By the end of 1841, however, they had a place of their own although one of its rooms wasn't quite finished. Any satisfaction that may have been felt at this necessary addition to the premises was tempered by the knowledge that years would elapse before it would be paid for. Debt seemed an almost inevitable accompaniment to building works in early non-conformity. At the end of 1843 it was reported that £46 - 13 - 3d (£46.66) was still owed on the chapel and £42 - 9 - 11d. (£42. 49) on the schoolroom. Two years later, however, the prospect brightened somewhat. Following the death of Mrs. Eddison of Gateford, her family offered to give £50 towards the liquidation of the debt, provided that the church raised the balance of what was owing within a year. No time was wasted in taking advantage of so generous an offer. An appeal was launched at a public tea meeting and the necessary amount was promised before its end, church members' contributions being, "liberally supported by friends present connected with the various other denominations of the town,"...[1] Few, if any, other families linked with the church could have matched the liberality of the Eddisons. They were prominent and influential in the town and district, Mr. Henry Eddison of Gateford being a well to do farmer.

Even though the financial situation had been eased for a while, it was not long before the church had to face a greater crisis. On the 31st August. 1848 Mr. Hugill submitted his resignation as pastor. This may not have been entirely unexpected as it had been clear for some time, perhaps, indeed for the whole period of his ministry, that he had been unhappy with denominational constraints and limitations in church organisation. "He was," he wrote, "convinced that Christians ought not to meet as 'Independents', nor as bound to conform to any merely human system whatever, but only as believers assembling in entire dependence on the Spirit of God and having the Scriptures as their only rule." [2] Not that his disquiet had caused acrimony in the church. In his letter of resignation he recalls, "the almost uninterrupted peace which we have enjoyed together," and adjudged his time in Worksop as, "the happiest period of my life." [3] Had Mr. Hugill left it at that and, in due course, moved away from the town, all would not have been too bad. He would have been sadly missed and gratefully remembered as an acceptable and diligent pastor. This, however, was not to be. Mr. Hugill chose to remain in Worksop and to establish his own church, meeting, at first, at his home and later in a building to be known throughout the town as "Hugill's chapel" and standing no more than a hundred yards from that of the Independents.[4] As was to be expected his continued presence had unfortunate consequences for his former church. No fewer than nineteen of its members defected to join him, leaving but twenty seven who remained loyal to their original cause.

Depleted in number and without a minister meant hard times and it was not until the end of the following year, 1849, that the gloom began to lighten. In December the Revd. George Swann was invited to undertake the pastorate. He was already acquainted with the church, having preached there on several occasions, but seemed to come with some reluctance. In the end, he appeared to balance the limitations of the small salary of £80 a year against the benefits of the, "salubrity of your climate," for his wife's delicate health and he began his ministry on the 1st January, 1850.

By the end of his first year membership had increased by ten and three months later a more accurate assessment of support was possible. The Religious Attendance Survey of the 30th March, 1851 revealed that about eighty attended morning service while twenty or so more were present in the evening. This compared more than favourably with the congregations of the Association Methodists and the Primitive Methodists though not with those of the Wesleyans where both services attracted around four hundred.

Mr. Swann's time of ministry was short. Somewhat unwilling to come, he didn't seem eager to stay and on the 5th December, 1852 he departed for Stafford. Perhaps a

When the Congregationalists built their Bridge Place Chapel in 1876, styles in design were changing. The plain fronted meeting house was no longer in favour. Chapels of the late 19th century were very often little different from Anglican churches of the same period. This Gothic appearance was certainly apparent at Worksop though the adjacent school room marks it out as a non-conformist place of worship. On this busy picture, it stands next to the premises of Ezra Taylor, the man who took the photograph.

hoped for increase of salary did not come up to his expectations. Whatever the reason, his replacement was not speedy and the church had to manage as best it could for just over three years without a leader. In the meantime services were taken by students or visiting ministers.

The interregnum was broken when the Revd. Elijah Pickford accepted the pastorate at the salary of £90 a year. That this was regarded as rather modest is suggested by an apologetic phrase in the letter of invitation. It read, (we are) "sorry that our present circumstances will not allow us to offer you more ...." As it was, Mr. Pickford only stayed for three years and while the interregnum that followed his departure was not particularly long, neither was the tenure of office of the next minister; both being measured in months.

The Gothic influence was evident in the interior of the Bridge Place Chapel too. Its arcades and lancet type windows could be found in many Anglican churches of the same period. A major difference was the prominent central pulpit in the chapel. The sermon was regarded as a key part of a non-conformist service and the preacher was always given a prominent place from which to deliver it.

When the next pastor, the Revd. John Stokes, was inducted on the 22nd. June, 1862 he came to a church where, over the past decade, periods of interregnum exceeded those of settled ministry. This must have been a disheartening time, perhaps one of faltering attendance and dwindling finances. Whatever the situation, things begun to improve under Mr. Stokes' leadership and after six months it was reported that the, "congregation was slowly but steadily improving and that peace and concord, abounded."[5] At the same time the, "highly prosperous condition of the Sunday School," was mentioned. Throughout 1863 a number of purchases were made that enhanced both the appearance of the interior of the chapel and the quality of worship. Cocoa nut matting was laid on the floor while, for use in communion services, a new flagon was bought and the old cups and plates electroplated. At the same time, the new Congregational Hymn Book was adopted and an organ bought. The former was interesting in that it indicated that, nationally at least, the old denominational name of Independent was being replaced by Congregational. Doubtless, locally, there would be some resistance to the change, particularly from members of long standing. The organ, which replaced a harmonium, cost £52 and, together with the new hymn books, helped towards more meaningful and enjoyable singing.

Unfortunately such a flurry of expenditure sadly depleted the church's finances. At the end of 1863 they had fallen to £2- 0 - 10d. (£2.04) and, making matters more serious, £17 was still owing on the organ. This was soon cleared, with a little to spare, when £19 - 9 s. (£19.45) was raised at a bazaar and, at the end of 1864, the treasurer was able to report that the church had £3 - 18 - 2d. (£3.91) in hand. This slightly larger amount does not mean that no further improvements were made. In November, 1864 as the early chill of winter was causing an occasional shiver in the congregation, it was decided to buy an additional stove.

Hopefully it was installed in time for the annual tea meeting which was held on the 2nd. February, 1865 for much was discussed and deliberations were doubtless protracted. Routine business apart, a matter described as a "great scandal" demanded immediate attention. A church member, a dedicated worker, a man of hitherto undoubted probity had been seen in the town in a state of drunkenness. As an immediate measure he was asked not to attend communion for a month but, although otherwise active in church matters, he clearly felt the shame that his lapse had occasioned for he wrote to the meeting, resigning his membership for a year. This was accepted though any sadness the consideration of the matter might have brought about was hastily dispelled by a subsequent decision of the meeting. It was resolved to hold a bazaar and tea meeting in the late spring with a view to using the proceeds as the start of a fund towards the cost of building a new chapel. This was later ratified and by the end of the year over £60 had been raised.

Despite its rather attractive appearance on the painting, members had, for some time, been expressing dissatisfaction with their chapel. Situated as it was, on Westgate, close to the poor and crowded housing of the Lead Hill area, it was hardly in one of the most fashionable parts of the town and it had been a long felt wish that one day they would be able to move to a site of greater prominence. In this aspiration they were supported by the Nottinghamshire Congregational Union, its secretary writing, "That this Association, taking into account the great importance of the town of Worksop and the very great need that exists for a new place of worship for the Congregational Church in that town in some eligible and commanding situation is rejoiced to know that the church in that place has already taken preliminary steps towards securing a suitable plot of ground." The Union assured the Worksop church of its support and of the likelihood of monetary help.

Apart from its seemingly ever present hand to mouth financial situation, the church in 1865 was in a reasonably healthy state. In the Revd. Mr. Stokes it had a settled and acceptable minister while its membership of thirty five was the highest that it had been for several years. Attendance was also growing, so much so that the pew opener was emboldened to ask for an increase of her quarterly pittance. It was agreed to allow her another half crown (12.5p) bringing the total up to £1. With steady support, a prevailing atmosphere of harmony and the prospect of a new chapel it was, indeed, an auspicious moment for the unknown artist to set up his easel and paint the picture that prompted these notes. The way to the new chapel proved long, protracted and, at times, disheartening. Finding and acquiring a suitable site was neither easy nor straight forward and, following the death of Mr. Stokes in 1869 and during the subsequent interregnum of nineteen months, enthusiasm flagged. It was revived in 1874 when the Revd. J.E. Moore became minister and, following his arrival on the 2nd. August, events moved with a hitherto unknown rapidity.

A site on Bridge Place was bought and on the 30th September, 1875 a memorial stone was laid by Mr. T.J. Pearson, a long time member, wise councillor and a generous benefactor of the church. Building work continued through the winter and by July of 1876 all was complete. The local paper[6] eulogised, "There is no doubt about its general sightliness, both outside and inside and the Congregationalists are to be congratulated upon the wonderful success they have achieved in being enabled to raise so commodious and handsome a structure in so short a time." On the 13th of that month, the opening service was held, described in the same paper as "a day of triumph."

On the Sunday following the opening, the 22nd. of July, a final service took place in the old chapel on Westgate, thus ending its forty five year story as the place of worship of the Independents, later called Congregationalists. It was vacated without regret, soon to be converted to a block of cottages and ultimately to be used as a store. It was demolished in 1972.

Notes and References

1. The Church Meeting Minute Book, 28th February, 1845.
2. Letter pasted in the church meeting minute book.
3. Ibid.
4. The building still stands on Lead Hill.
5. The Church Meeting Minute Book, 2nd. January, 1863.
6. The Retford and Gainsborough Times, 15th July, 1876.

PICTURE SUPPLEMENT, 2
FIRE AT EYRE'S.

Unable to sleep, Mrs. W. Hayes, looked out of her bedroom window at ten past three on the morning of 18th July, 1911. She noticed that a fire had broken out in Eyre's furniture shop which stood on Newcastle Street, just about opposite the Wesleyan Chapel. The alarm was raised and the Worksop fire engine was soon on the scene. It was later joined by the engine from Welbeck Abbey. Together they fought the flames and it was not until two o'clock in the afternoon that the fire was completely extinguished.

The damage was total. All that remained was an empty shell. Apart from a few pieces of furniture that had been removed before the fire was at its fiercest, the rest of the stock, valued at £4000, was destroyed. Above the shop, the first floor of the building, which was used by the Pelham Lodge of Freemasons was similarly devastated. Regalia, records and artefacts of the order, all succumbed to the flames. Even the doors of the Wesleyan Chapel, across the road, were singed by the heat.

Fires usually attract crowds and this occasion was no exception. In this picture, taken by Ezra Taylor, the Worksop and Welbeck engines have been parked close to the Town Dyke Bridge on Bridge Street so that water could be pumped from the River Ryton to supplement the supply from the mains. Behind the crowd, the property known as the Arcade is incomplete, just the northernmost five units have been finished with the arcading in position.

Matriarch of the Chairmakers.

Sometime in 1822 John Gabbitas, who lived at Gamston, loaded his belongings and the tools of his trade onto a cart and, with his wife Elizabeth, moved the few miles to Worksop where he settled on the Common, the present day Eastgate. Not only did he bring with him all his worldly possessions but he also introduced a new trade into the town for he was a chairmaker. Soon, he, his younger brother Henry, a handful of local men and one or two apprentices were producing Windsor chairs, a type of furniture which was to be made in Worksop for the next hundred years.

This chair was made shortly after Elizabeth Gabbitas had taken over the management of the family firm, following the death of her husband in 1839. Made around 1840, it was solidly constructed, was meant to last and is still in regular use today.

Elizabeth Gabbitas re-married in 1843. After a few years she retired leaving the firm in the hands of her brother-in-law. It remained in business until 1853 though members of the Gabbitas family continued to make chairs until later in the century

Four years before he moved to Worksop, John Gabbitas had married Elizabeth, a young eighteen year old girl. She was a farmer's daughter and came from Owston in The Isle of Axholme. One who knew her described her as possessing, "a fine well-knit frame, a sound constitution, and a large amount of Yorkshire shrewdness of character."[1] These qualities were to serve her well as, from its early days she was the guiding hand behind the business. No doubt her husband could make good chairs but he appears to have been an easy going man, competent in the workshop but less so in his dealings with customers. It was fortunate that he had such a wife behind him who, it was stated, "was from the start the 'better man' in the business.[2]

This involvement could not have been easy, especially in the early days as Elizabeth also had a young family to care for. Her eldest son, Peter, was born in the year of their coming to Worksop, Louisa five years later and Frederick in 1831. Both boys followed their father's trade. At thirteen, Peter had to earn at least 10s. (50p) a week: anything over that he could keep for himself.[3] Later, after failing in business on his own account, he moved to Bristol where he became quite well known as a poet, much of his verse advocating temperance, a cause, so it was said, that was instilled into him at his father's knee. Frederick remained a chairmaker in his home town. Despite her many domestic reponsibilities, Elizabeth gave much of her time to the business. "She held it together with great ability,"[4] so it was written, "managed it more and more as she found her husband became less constant in his business habits and eventually she had complete control".

This did not just entail keeping an eye on the men, ordering necessary stock and carrying out the basic office work, Elizabeth took a much more active and strenuous part than that. She went out from Worksop and sought custom far and wide, travelling into Yorkshire, Derbyshire, Lincolnshire and Lancashire. This was in pre-railway days and the discomforts and hazards that she experienced can well be imagined. Such arduous work would have daunted many a man but Elizabeth Gabbitas stuck to it, obtaining the necessary orders, collecting all the money that was owing and, no doubt, looking on with no little satisfaction as the chairs that she had sold were piled high onto waiting wagons, ready for their journey to distant parts.

From August, 1839 what had been generally understood became a recognized fact for on the 26th of that month John Gabbitas died and Elizabeth became head of the firm. John was but forty two years old. Her brother in law, Henry, looked after the workshop in place of John but otherwise things continued very much as before. However, one little change was introduced. Instead of chairs being' marked I. Gabbitas on the bottom of the seat they were now stamped E. Gabbitas on the back edge. Very few of the former are known to have survived while examples of the latter are quite numerous. This was rather puzzling as, until recently, it was thought that Elizabeth too had died within a few years of her husband, perhaps around 1843.

Death, however, is not the only cause of a woman's seeming disappearance from her known surroundings. Elizabeth chose a far happier way of baffling future historians:

she re-married and thereafter became Mrs. Elizabeth Thorpe. Her second husband, Henry, was a mason and six years her junior. Evidence, scanty as it is, suggests that she continued to manage the family business for several more years though by 1851 she had clearly handed over to her brother in law. In the census returns of that year he is recorded as a master chairmaker employing nine men, three boys and three apprentices. This was the largest establishment of its kind in Worksop.

Elizabeth's influence was not confined to her own firm, it permeated the trade in the town. This was through the lads who began their working lives as apprentices with Gabbitas's and who set up on their own account when they had served their time. Their names form a roll call of Worksop's chairmakers. One of the first, and subsequently one of the best known, was Isaac Allsop, affectionately known as Ike by Mrs. Gabbitas, Others included Joseph, John and Charles Godfrey, Benjamin Gilling and Frederick Hoggard. All these men learnt their chairmaking skills in the Eastgate workshop where also, hopefully, some of the drive, determination and business ability of Mrs. Gabbitas rubbed off onto them too. They would be better men if it did.

Sometime during the later 1840's Elizabeth and her second husband left Worksop and took a farm on the Derbyshire side of Sheffield. They stayed there for about twenty years and throughout that time Elizabeth travelled into Sheffield each week to stand on the market. There the skills of salesmanship that she had developed in disposing of her chairs no doubt helped her to build up a regular custom for her butter, cheese and eggs. When retirement beckoned the couple returned to Worksop and spent their final years on Eastgate. Dates are difficult but they were certainly living there by the time of the 1871 census. It was there, too, that both of them died, Henry Thorpe in 1882 and Elizabeth at the end of 1884. She was eighty five.

By then, the trade that she and her first husband had brought into Worksop was edging into decline. Although her son Frederick, her nephew Robert and his son Thomas were still making chairs, they were for other masters. The family firm, for which she had worked so hard and for so long, had closed, probably following the death of Henry in May of 1858. Another sign of the times was that while Thomas followed his father in the trade, his five brothers sought elsewhere for their livelihoods. They became coalminers. At the end of the century, just a handful of men worked as chairmakers. Within a few years the two remaining firms, those of William Gilling and William Bramer, had closed leaving just one man as sole survivor of the trade in the town. He was John Kelk who, as a lad had served his apprenticeship with Isaac Allsop who, in his turn, was an apprentice of John and Elizabeth Gabbitas. Just three generations spanned the coming, the growth and the end of chairmaking in the town. Those who practised the trade are now all but forgotten though their legacy remains. A good number of their chairs still exist: chairs originally priced in shillings but now valued in hundreds of pounds. Some bear their maker's names, and those stamped E. Gabbitas, Worksop, ought to remind their owners of a remarkable woman, a pioneer and a mainstay of the trade, "who deserves to be remembered by the people of Worksop."[5]

Notes and References

1. The Retford and Gainsborough Times, 2 January, 1885. The county attribution appears to be incorrect, as Owston is in Lincolnshire.

2. Ibid.

3. The Nottinghamshire Countryside, Summer, 1964. "Looking Back" by Gordon M. Clarke.

4. The Retford and Gainsborough Times, 2 January, 1885.

5. Ibid.

PICTURE SUPPLEMENT, 3
EYRE'S. NEW PREMISES.

Burnt out of their Newcastle Street shop on the 18th July, 1911, Eyre's were back in business by the 22nd. of the same month. Standing empty at the top of Bridge Street in a prime position, were the premises shown on this picture. They had recently been vacated by D. J. Smith, draper, who had moved to a shop already completed in the Arcade buildings.

With a speed that almost defies belief the premises were acquired by Eyre's, cleaned, stocked, and were open for business within four days. As they boast on the picture, they were long regarded as the premier house furnishers in the town. As he writes these words, the author is sitting on a chair that was bought from Eyre's over sixty years ago. The firm is still in business though, while retaining the original name, is under different ownership.

Like Carthorses.....Like Greyhounds.

Sometime during the 1950's the Worksop Guardian ran a series of articles under the title of "Worksop's Staple Industry". They were written by the late Mr. Edwin Topham, then quite elderly and whose memory ran back many years to the last quarter of the 19th century. Although by that time, more local men worked at Shireoaks and Steetley collieries than in any other occupation, the sweet aroma of roasting malt still pervaded the air, as it had for centuries, and fully justified in Mr. Topham's mind his description of malting as the town's staple industry.

During the first half of the 19th century there were upwards of thirty maltings in or around Worksop. Most were small, operated by the maltster with, perhaps, one man to help him. One of the smallest, shown in this picture, stood by the roadside at Gateford. This photograph was taken in 1967 long after its working days were over. The wooden cowl that topped the pyramid shaped roof of the kiln had collapsed just a few years earlier.

It was then an occupation that had certainly been followed for at least two hundred and fifty years and most likely for many more. In 1636 John Harrison compiled a survey of the town for the Earl of Arundel and Surrey who then owned much property in it. He noted an occasional "kilnehouse" and in one instance he was more specific. Close to "Brassebridge Mill" was a "kilne and Maulthouse". Further early references to malting are infrequent though in 1722 a Bawtry man, apprehensive that improvements to the River Don would lead to a decrease in trade along the Idle, mentioned in a letter that the carts that brought lead to the wharves of his home town, took back into Derbyshire "great quantities" of malt from Mansfield and Worksop.[1] Whatever trade by road there may have been was supplemented after 1777 when the Chesterfield Canal was opened. Although never a principal cargo of the horse drawn narrow boats, the fact that maltings were built on the canal side is a sure sign that the new waterway was of benefit to the town's maltsters. Its convenience certainly stimulated a growth of malting in the town.

A directory of the early 1820's[2] mentions no fewer than thirty two maltsters, by far the greatest number of people following a single occupation. Worksop's staple industry indeed. At least eleven of these kilns were said to be on the Common, the northern part of the town in close proximity to the canal. The rest were distributed fairly evenly in other parts. There were six in Radford, four along Potter Street and two on each of Bridge Street, Park Street, Castle Street and close to the market. None were large. In size they were comparable with workshops rather than factories, worked by the maltster on his own or with one or two labourers. In scale they harmonised with their neighbouring buildings though in one way they stood out from them. This was in the shape of the roof of the kiln. Very often it was pyramidal and it was always crowned with a cowl through which the pungent vapour from the roasting malt rose into the surrounding air. People passing through commented on this distinctive feature of the townscape. One such person wrote of, "the great number of maltkilns standing about in every direction. Whatever others may think, to my eyes these structures are rather picturesque than unpleasing objects, partly from their general construction, but principally from the appearance of their cowls, as the wooden turn-about hoods on their roofs are termed."[3]

Nearly all of these small, early buildings have long since disappeared though those

Another early maltings stood on Eastgate. Like others of similar age, it was built of stone and had a pantile roof. This photograph was taken in 1963, after it had been abandoned for some years and shortly before its demolition. Just visible in the background is a later and much larger maltings that was built in 1876. It stood by the railway and was able to make use of that form of transport.

whose memory of the town goes back thirty or forty years may remember one in derelict condition on the north side of Eastgate and another by the roadside at Gateford. They were both built of stone and had pantile roofs, the latter retaining vestiges of its wooden cowl until the early 1960s. One may, however, still survive though it is heavily disguised, its original purpose hidden behind a modern shop front. It stands on Bridge Place, older townspeople will remember it as Dougill's, the ladies' outfitters.[4] Go into the Netherholme car park and look at it from there and it presents a very different aspect. There is the unmistakable form of an early malt house, its stone walls, pantile roof and the adjacent kiln making odd neighbours to the assortment of later buildings that hem them in. Others of the same materials and similar size though perhaps of even greater antiquity have long since gone. One such stood on Castle Street, just behind the buildings that faced Bridge Street. A young man who worked in one of the neighbouring shops watched its demolition and noticed piles of malting tiles among the debris. It was his opinion that the building dated from the 16th century at the latest.[5] Another kiln of similar age stood on the corner of Netherton Road and Newgate Street. When it was taken down in 1905 a passer by was amazed at the massiveness of the internal timbers, they reminded him of the "wooden walls of old England".[6]

Such were the maltings of early 19th century Worksop. Small in size, traditional in appearance and in their mode of working, seasonal in operation and non-intensive in man power and yet productive of wealth out of all proportion to such considerations. Their level of prosperity can be measured, at least in part, by the amount of malt tax that was paid. In 1821 there were about forty maltsters in Worksop and district and they paid no less than £51,022 in tax..[7]

This hated imposition was introduced in 1697 and was in force until 1880. It was rated at so much per bushel of malt produced and in the 1820s it hovered around the 2 shillings (IOp) mark. Thereafter the amount tended to fall though by the 1850's, during the Crimean War, it increased to 4 shillings (20p) a bushel. This variation of rate made it unreliable to judge the state of the trade in the town by the annual amount paid in tax. Such figures, though, do suggest a decline in the second quarter of the century as £36,639 was paid in 1825 and £36,596 in 1851 However, these are still considerable sums and a commentator does add, "their years payments to the excise are seldom less than £30,000."[8]

There is, though, other evidence suggesting that the town's maltsters were not enjoying such good days during the 1830's and 1840's. One of these signs is that fewer were in business. From the mid-thirties in 1832, the number had fallen to around twenty five in 1844 and to seventeen in 1852.[9] Backing up this impression of recession in trade, Edwin Eddison, in his History of Worksop of 1854 commented that malting, "had somewhat declined." This was but temporary and by the time that Eddison's book appeared the amount paid in malt duty again topped £40,000. In fact, he went on to state that the town, "paid more in malt duty, we are told, than any other place in the kingdom, with one exception - the town of Ware." That claim, perhaps would not stand too close an examination. Newark would certainly challenge it.

Another sign of less profitable times is the quite heavy change over in the ownership of the maltings. Of the thirty or so known maltsters in 1822, at least a dozen were out of business by 1832 and of those trading in that year, the names of around twenty do not appear in the directory of 1844. Of course, all would not have left the trade for economic reasons. Death and infirmity must have taken their toll but, never the less, the change in ownership was considerable. It is difficult to be precise about numbers as the two sources of information - the trade directories and the census returns - rarely, if ever, tally. As an example of this, the former never mention Godfrey Dethick which the latter of 1881 include as a master maltster, employing one man. There are other discrepancies, too.

It is doubtful if anyone remembers Netherholme other than as a run-down and semi-ruinous building. This is a shame as, for many years, it was a handsome town house, standing in its own extensive grounds on the west side of Bridge Place. For a time it was the home of Samuel Watkins, a well to do maltster and a man who was prominent in town affairs.

Most of Worksop's maltsters of the first half of the 19th century survive as little more than names. Their ages, sparse family details and an address, though whether that of their home or work place isn't always clear, are the only other pieces of information about them. Just a few, however, emerge more fully from the past. One of these is Samuel Watkins. He was born in 1791: one source says at Uppingham in Rutland, another at Southwark. By 1820 he was married and living at Worksop and sometime during that decade he set up as a maltster, an occupation that he was to follow until well into the

1860's. At first, though, his commitment to malting was only part time as he was also estate agent for the Duke of Norfolk. After 1840, when the Duke sold his Worksop Manor estate, he would have more time for his maltings which was one of the group that clustered along the canal side on Bridge Place. Although it only needed a work force of two, it was obviously sufficiently profitable to allow him to take a prominent part in town affairs and to provide a comfortable way of life for his family. Living at first on Potter Street, he later moved to Netherholme, a substantial house in its own grounds on the west side of Bridge Place between the river and the canal. It was described as, "one of the nicest houses in Worksop, and is pleasantly situated in the centre of the town."[10] Containing three living rooms, a kitchen and other service rooms on the ground floor and six bedrooms above it would certainly provide adequate accommodation for the family and plenty of work for the resident house maid. Long time Worksop residents may recall the house in its latter days, neglected and derelict before it was demolished to make way for the shopping precinct that for a while bore its name. Samuel Watkins was as familiar a figure at committee meetings as he was in his malt kiln as he took an active interest in all municipal matters. In 1840 he was treasurer of the committee that arranged the activities to celebrate the queen's wedding. Four years later he served first on the provisional committee and then on the executive committee of the Sheffield and Lincolnshire Junction Railway. Later in the year he was made a provisional director of the company.

Within the town he was a member of the Board of Guardians that administered the workhouse and poor relief in the district and in 1856 he was elected a member of the recently formed Local Board of Health, the town council of the day. Age did nothing to diminish such interests and in 1862, when he was in his seventies, he was appointed to a committee to consider ways of increasing church accommodation in the town. This led to the building of St. John's church in 1869 which, sadly, Samuel Watkins never saw as he died towards the end of September of 1864.

Another maltster to emerge in some detail from the past is Edward Baxter. He was born in 1828 and followed his father to the kiln. By the time he was twenty one he had set up in business on his own. His kiln was on Bridge Place and for much of his life he lived nearby on Bridge Street, moving latterly to Ashley House on Carlton Road. Though in the business in a middling way, he only employed five men at the most, he was highly respected and regarded as, "one of the bulwarks of the trade."[11] Like Samuel Watkins, his influence spread beyond the doors of his maltings for he was active in many aspects of town life. He served on the Local Board of Health, for a time as its chairman, the position he also held with the Worksop Corn Exchange and Market Company. For many years too he was one of the managers and, latterly, a trustee of the Worksop Savings Bank while the church was another cause to which he generously devoted his time. He was a churchwarden at the Priory, he sat on the committee that led to the building of St. John's church and, following its opening, he held office as churchwarden there. Impressive as this list seems, it wasn't all for Edward Baxter was also a founder member

This is a better view of the railway side maltings glimpsed on a previous photograph. It was built in 1876 for John Preston, a local maltster. It shows the change that took place in the second half of the 19th century from buildings of an earlier date. Built of brick, it was larger in size and more factory like in appearance. Even so, it only needed eight men to work it.

of the Pelham Lodge of Freemasons, being for two periods its Worshipful Master. As befitted men engaged in its staple industry, Samuel Watkins and Edward Baxter loomed large in the life of the town. Known to everyone, any organisation or cause that gained their support would regard itself as fortunate. Less is known of other master maltsters though doubtless some would be similarly involved in civic, church and social activities.

1849 marked a turning point in the story of malting in Worksop. Prior to that year all the maltings had been small or middling in size. Work was but seasonal and once the local crops of barley had been dealt with the workers had to seek other employment until the next harvest. This only involved a few men and in most maltings the owner took off his jacket and worked alongside his labourers. The 16th July, 1849 was the actual date that led to a change in this centuries old way of working and organization, as on that day trains began running along the newly built Manchester, Sheffield and Lincolnshire Railway. For the maltings this meant that barley could be brought in from a much wider area, thus lengthening the working season and providing the labourers with a job that lasted for the greater part of the year.

First to take advantage of the railway was the Manchester brewer John M. Threlfall. By 1852 the large Clinton maltings just north of the line was in full production. Every four days, for nine months of the year, three hundred quarters of barley[12] were wetted down as the first stage in the malting process. In contrast with this, when one of the older, more traditional maltings in Abbey Street was advertised for sale in 1874 it was stated that its capacity was thirteen quarters every four days.[13] Where the Clinton led, others followed. In 1876, a local man, John Preston, who had previously been in business in a smaller way had a large, new maltings built on Eastgate by the side of the railway. So convivial was the supper that marked the opening that, "several persons had to be conveyed by a kind hearted man home in a handy and friendly wheelbarrow."[14] Other large factory-like maltings were built by Sheffield brewers, one around 1875 by Thomas Berry by the railway at the top of Sherwood Road and one in 1880 for William Stones on Gateford Road. This last date is not without significance. In that year the hated malt tax was repealed. Henceforth maltsters would not have to pay 2s. 8d (13p) for every bushel of malt that they produced and would doubtless consider the times propitious for expansion. The larger maltings clearly needed more men to work them though the numbers were still comparatively small. John Preston only employed eight men at his new kiln on Eastgate. This was the smallest of the more recent buildings and Mr. Preston would still be a well known person to his workmen. They would see him in the maltings and greet him about the town. In contrast, it is doubtful if Mr. Threlfall was ever a familiar figure at the Clinton kilns or Mr. Stones at Gateford Road. They were more concerned with the supervision of their breweries and left the running of their Worksop maltings to managers. Thus, in 1885, one maltster's manager and two foremen maltsters are recorded in a local directory.[15]

Never labour intensive, this picture shows the workforce of Stone's maltings on Gateford Road, posing for their photograph in 1905. Several have the tools of their work with them, both wooden and metal shovels, a fork, brush and watering can, while the men seated second right and at the left end of the row illustrate that refreshment was frequently necessary for those working in the heat of the kiln.

However large or however new the maltings, the method of converting the barley into malt remained the same. Whether a man worked in the oldest, smallest kiln in the town or in one of the latest to be built, his tasks and the way he carried them out did not differ. Malting involved three basic processes: steeping, flooring and roasting. All were simple in themselves though great care was needed in matters of timing and temperature control. First of all, the barley was soaked in long troughs or cisterns called steeps. There it remained for three days or more, the grains swelling as they absorbed the water.

Maltings were graded according to the amount of barley that they could steep at any one time. The extent of the trade in the town in the early 1870's can be appreciated from the statistic that throughout the six to seven month malting season, one thousand and thirty nine quarters of barley were steeped every four days.[16] Converting this to tonnage, it equals upwards of nine thousand and three hundred for the season, about three quarters of which was brought into the town by rail. Another piece of information that can be deduced from the steeping capacity is the possible work force as it was said that one man was required for every fifteen quarters that was laid down.[17] By this reckoning, the smallest kilns could be worked by the master maltster on his own while the Clinton needed at least twenty men. A similar calculation suggests that a minimum of around seventy men worked in the town's maltings.

When the barley had been sufficiently steeped, the troughs were drained and the grain shovelled out and spread onto the working floor of the maltings. There it lay at a varying depth, depending on the kiln temperature, for up to a fortnight until germination was judged to be sufficiently advanced. During the flooring process, the grain was periodically worked, the men using the traditional wooden shovels or wooden tined forks or even rakes. From the floor the grain was taken to the kiln for roasting, the final process in its transformation to malt.

The kiln floor was made of square tiles, each perforated with groups of holes, small at the top to prevent the grain falling through and wider underneath to admit maximum heat from the fire that burnt below. A usual job for a young lad starting work in a maltings was to poke the holes in the tiles clear of any blockages that may have formed during firing. Kilning usually took two or three days and as the grain had to be turned each day in a temperature rising to around 200 degrees Fahrenheit, the local saying arose that the men started the season like cart horses and finished it like greyhounds. Even more unpleasant than that was the final process of the malting operation. This was screening, in which any impurities were removed from the malt. Not only was the heat still intense but the dust that arose was so thick that even the hardiest could only work for a short time without relief.

Mr. C.E. Christian spent the greater part of his working life in the local maltings and, in his later days, recalled how these three basic processes were carried out in the town. "Barley was taken in from the local farms," he wrote, "and stored until the colder weather, then a batch of it was soaked for several days in long troughs called "steeps". The grain was then thrown out and spread several inches thick on the dim, cool floors. The maltster's labourers daily turned the grain until the master maltster decided the germination of the grain had gone on for just the right period - usually just over a week.

"Then the golden barley, now swollen and showing tiny rootlets, was loaded by sheer hard work on to the floor of the tiled upstairs kiln. A fire of coal and coke dried the grain, driving the "reek" or vapour out through the cowl-topped kiln. For three to four days the grain was turned by the sweating maltsters, and the final "curing" period, requiring something like 200 F., gave the grain the right colour - pale for light ale and dark for mild ale. All the time the team of maltsters, toiled for daily short periods in the hot kiln. Then they would finally enter it again and throw the malted barley into hoppers or bins."[18]

The tools with which the maltings' workers carried out their various tasks changed little over the years. They were simple yet functional; mainly of wood, products of the local timber yards. Principal among them was the shovel which was something of a status symbol as well as a mere tool of the trade as the size of the blade was supposedly indicative of the strength of the owner. With these shovels the barley was moved between the different stages of the malting process and the grain turned during flooring and kilning.

Towards the end of the century, Mr. H.P. Forrest, a Worksop ironmonger and agricultural implement maker, introduced a shovel with a metal blade. This found scant favour with the workmen who, rather disdainfully, referred to them as tin shovels and only used them for moving the dry grain. Nevertheless, a man, albeit on the back row, is holding one in the group photograph taken in 1905 of the workers at Stones' maltings on Gateford Road. Another is shouldering a wooden fork while a third has a wide headed brush, no doubt used when moving the grain from one process to the next. Sometimes, if it was felt necessary to speed up germination, the grain was sprinkled as it lay on the floor, hence the watering can on the picture. The smaller cans held by two of the men were for their allocation of beer, compensation for working in the extreme heat of the kiln. An idea of the full yet small range of tools and tackle needed in malting can be gained from the advertisement[19] of a sale following the death in 1878 of Mr. Tom. Wilson of Carlton Road. Apart from two Avery weighing machines, the rest of the items on offer have an ageless sound to them. They included four turning shovels, two five grain forks, two iron grain rakes, two malt screens, three grain barrows, two running barrows, two boobys (barrows),[20] coke shovels, drum bushel with strickles (a drum shaped measure holding one bushel with sticks to level its contents at the top), upwards of five hundred four and six bushel sacks, skeps and other oddments.

With such tools, malting was never less than hard physical work though the introduction of some mechanisation to the newest and largest maltings did ease slightly the lot of those employed in them. With the building of these more modern kilns in the last quarter of the 19th century, the industry reached its height of prosperity. In 1876 the local paper commented, "Among the improvements which are continually seen going on in Worksop is the building of new malt kilns on a scale not only of magnitude, but in a style calculated to improve the looks of the town. Whatever else in the matter of trade flags in the town, the malting business goes on and increases." The writer ends his report with the invocation, "O be joyful unto malt."[21]

While there were those who may well have been joyful unto malt, all was not as rosy as the saying might suggest. Even in the latest maltings, work was still seasonal and for three or four months of the year the men had to seek alternative employment. This was because temperature was a key factor in malting and the summer months were judged too warm for successful working. Thus in a good year the maltings would be in operation from September until about May, depending upon the availability of grain and the demand for malt. Other circumstances could restrict production too and of these fire was an ever present danger as both the buildings and their contents were particularly vulnerable to its ravages.

One of the most devastating, and spectacular, took place on the evening of the 8th March, 1881. At quarter to nine the western end of Messrs. Thomas Berry and Co's Station Maltings was seen to be on fire. This was the part of the building where the processed malt was screened and stored. Soon the flames, fanned by a westerly wind, burst through the roof and rose into the night sky. Within half an hour the Worksop Fire Brigade arrived and concentrated its efforts on trying to prevent the fire from spreading to the rest of the building. At first this seemed a hopeless task and help was called for from the Welbeck Abbey and the Sheffield brigades. The latter was the first to arrive, the engine being loaded onto a truck at Victoria station. This was coupled to the next train bound for Worksop. By the time the Welbeck engine galloped up Carlton Road the fire was under control and Mr. Berry was surveying the burnt out debris of the affected part of his maltings. Almost seven thousand quarters of malt had been destroyed together with machinery and equipment. His losses, he estimated, were between ten and twelve thousand pounds.[22]

Stretching along the south side of the railway, three storeys high for much of its length, five at its eastern end, the Station kilns was one of Worksop's largest and certainly its most imposing maltings. It is perhaps not surprising that it was also one of the first in the town to break the working traditions of centuries and introduce a degree of mechanisation into its production methods. In October of 1901 a correspondent from the local paper visited the maltings and was shown round by Mr. Simonds, the manager. Much of the work was still manual and it was not until the kilns were reached that the improvements were apparent. A newly fitted gas powered engine drove machinery which considerably reduced the time that the men needed to be in the kilns to turn the roasting malt. Hitherto it took them almost one and a quarter hours to carry out

Thomas Berry, a Sheffield brewer, had the imposing Station Maltings built during the 1870's. Its construction marked the high point of Worksop as a malting centre. As in all maltings, fire was a constant hazard, a most spectacular and destructive blaze taking place in 1881 when the Sheffield fire engine had to be despatched by train to help combat it. This photograph shows the maltings in its later days, in 1965.

the task; the new apparatus reduced this time to half an hour. "Messrs. Berry have introduced this machinery," so the report stated, "in consideration of the health and comfort of the workmen." Another innovation added further to that well being. This was a fan that was installed in the screening room. Revolving at well over a thousand times a minute, it helped to keep some of the dust away from the eyes and noses of the workmen, making an extremely uncomfortable job just a little more bearable. The reporter was highly impressed with all that he saw and concluded his article, "that it is one of the cleanest malt houses I have ever visited."[23]

Despite the hard nature of the work and its attendant discomforts, the maltings' labourer tended to stick to his job. Mr. C.E. Christian commented that, "after being paid off, directly the season was to begin, most of them were back for another winter of sweating and toiling in the malthouses of the town."[24] Clearly a camaraderie developed, as so often does among those who share in the same demanding work. In some maltings this feeling was further strengthened by occasional social events that provided a brief pleasurable interlude between hours with the shovel and at the screens. Thus, early in 1878, the annual supper of the employees of the Clinton maltings was held, the tables being set up in part of the building where the men carried out their daily work. In spite of this association, the evening was thoroughly enjoyable. An account reports that, "The 'spread' was ample and a good one, to which full justice was done." On the removal of the cloth, Mr. James Wilson, the manager, occupied the chair and Mr. Lee, the foreman maltster, the vice chair and the usual protocol of speeches, toasts and songs filled out the rest of the evening. Works outings were not unknown and in 1872 the men from the same maltings, with their families, spent the day at Liverpool. They travelled by special train, enjoyed a steamer trip into the Irish Sea and spent some time on the beach at Eastham. After a very full day they arrived back at Worksop at midnight.[25]

Such social occasions were not limited to the workmen: the maltsters sat together round the table too. In 1850 their annual supper was held at the Wheatsheaf Inn and forty two were present. Most of these men owned or rented their own premises: just a few managed the maltings of non-working owners. Their number gives an idea of how many maltings there were in the town and its immediate vicinity in the last years before the coming of the large factory-like kilns. It is good to read that these master maltsters spent their evening, "in a very agreeable and comfortable manner,"[26] for within two years of their repast the walls of the Clinton kilns were rising on the northern side of the railway lines. This, as has already been stated, marked the beginning of the transformation of the industry in the town.

Some of those men who dined, at the Wheatsheaf would soon be forced out of business by competition from the larger kilns. Not that this decrease was drastic. Many people living in the town at the time would hardly be aware of it. Numbers as recorded in the various directories can only be regarded as approximate but they do indicate the trend. By the early 1860's there were at least twenty four maltsters in business. Twenty years later this had fallen to seventeen and by the end of the century to fourteen. Despite this decline, the trade still bore a healthy face. In 1901, looking back over the past one hundred years, the local paper wrote, "The malting trade, during the century, has been at a high water mark," and continued, "the town is still a great place for malting. The Worksop and Retford Brewery Company (a flourishing industry in itself) owns many active kilns and besides these there are the Clinton Kilns, Mr. John Preston's, Messrs. Berry's, Mr. F. Foster's, Messrs. T. and J. Preston's and others."[27]

Such comments suggested a promising future and for a while seemed fully justified but, as the years slipped by technological change made the Worksop maltings less competitive in an ever shifting market. The smaller independently owned kilns were the first to succumb to the new challenges that faced the industry. By the mid-twentieth century only the four largest undertakings were still in business and, sadly, their days were numbered. The one on the railway side, neighbour for many years to Godley and Goulding's timber yard, and latterly owned by Edward Sutcliffe, Ltd. was the first to close. Two fires, one in 1966 and the other in 1969 accelerated the closure of the Station kilns which occurred in 1976.

The Clinton maltings which had striven to keep pace with technological improvements by installing a self tipping kiln and building a vast new silo, ceased production at about the same time. A similar fate befell the maltings on Gateford Road, originally built for Stones the Sheffield brewers and subsequently the property of Bass Charrington (North) Ltd. Although still producing around three thousand tons of malt a year it was not considered economically viable and so, on the 12th September, 1970, the seventeen employees worked their final shift, laid down their shovels and made their ways home for the last time.

Thus Worksop's long time 'staple' industry was no more. The wisps of vapour rising from the cowls of the kilns and the aroma of the roasting barley would be no more than a memory. Just as wind and water mills had ceased to provide the flour for our daily bread, so the local maltings no longer produced the vital ingredient for the nightly pint. Evidence on the ground of so widespread and long established an industry does not disappear overnight and today, over twenty years after the last maltings closed, a dozen or so of the buildings remain, some altered out of all recognition, others retaining their basic features. At least ten survive as substantial buildings while odd fragments of wall indicate the whereabouts of one or two others. Easiest identified is one set back a hundred yards or so from the west side of Gateford Road, between Grafton Street and the railway. The observant eye can pick out three more on, or near to, Gateford Road, two on Eastgate and one each on Clarence Road, Carlton Road, Bridge Place and Potter Street. As long as some of these remain, Worksop will have reminders of an industry that spanned centuries of the town's story, that in its heyday, brought in considerable wealth and provided work which, though arduous, engendered a feeling of satisfaction, even pride, in those who carried it out.

Notes and References

1. T.S. Willan. The Early History of the Don Navigation.

2. Pigot's London and Provincial Directory, 1822/'23.

3. John Holland. History of Worksop. 1826.

4. It is now (2004) occupied by the shops of Incraft, Marshalls and Shoefayre.

5. Undated cutting from an article by "Roger de Busli" in the Worksop Guardian.

6. Undated cutting from the Worksop Guardian.

7. White's Directory of Nottinghamshire, 1832.

8. Ibid.

9. These figures are taken from White's Directories of those years.

10. The Retford and Gainsborough Times, 21 September, 1888.

11. Ibid. 10 June, 1887.

12. A quarter of barley weighs 448 pounds.

13. The Retford and Gainsborough Times, 5 December, 1874.

14. Ibid. 22 April, 1876.

15. White's Directory of Nottinghamshire, 1885.

16. The Mansfield Reporter, 4 November, 1870.

17. Jonathan Brown. Steeped in Tradition.

18. The Worksop Trader, 8 October, 1980.

19. The Retford and Gainsborough Times, 18 October, 1878.

20. Probably a corruption of bobys, a type of barrow manufactured and patented by Robert Boby of Bury St. Edmunds.

21. The Retford and Gainsborough Times, 8 April, 1876.

22. Ibid. 11 March, 1881.

23. The Worksop Guardian, 11 October, 1901

24. The Worksop Trader, 8 October, 1980.

25. The Retford and Gainsborough Times, 31 August, 1872.

26. The Nottingham Review, 18 January, 1850.

27. The Worksop Guardian, 11 January, 1901.

William "Potter" Ward.

William Ward certainly wasn't born with a silver spoon in his mouth. In fact, it is extremely doubtful if such an item of cutlery ever came his way throughout his long life. Poverty loomed over him all his days and was only kept at bay by hard work and an indomitable spirit.

He was born on the 3rd. of May, 1839 in a house on Newgate Street that stood almost opposite the end of Vicars Walk. His father, Jack, worked on Castle Farm for a basic wage of 12s. (60p) a week while his mother, Mary, was a member of the Layhe family, long established and well known in Worksop. When William was four his parents moved to Sheffield, doubtless hoping for better prospects in one of the factories there.

William Ward looks quite dapper on this photograph as he poses with one of his donkeys, with which he hawked his pots to towns and villages up to a forty mile radius of Worksop. This he did for forty years until retiring in 1912 at the age of 72. He was a popular figure in the town, often announcing his approach by loud and tuneful whistling, a skill by which he was widely known. (Picture by permission of Roz.and Ian Davies.)

These were not realised and after about twelve months the family returned to Worksop, In that pre-railway age they travelled by carrier's cart, a slow, lumbering vehicle operated by Mr. William Barlow of the French Horn Inn. He was a well known local personality, famed in his younger days as a prize fighter, and one of the last men in the town to wear a smock frock, gaiters and buckled shoes.

Until they could find a home of their own, the young family lived with Mr. Ward's father in Bedlam Square. This oddly and somewhat ominously named property stood to the south of Castle Street and consisted of a dozen small cottages, badly built and

"Bedlam Square" off Castle Street, even before it attained this abandoned look, was amongst Worksop's poorest housing in the middle years of the 19th century. It was here that the young William Ward lived for a short time when his family returned to town after a spell in Sheffield. Standing in the centre of the group is Cal Crow (Caroline Moore) who earned her unusual name from her occupation. She was a bird scarer.

in a sad state of repair. It was an insalubrious area in which few would choose to live and, fortunately, the Ward family's stay was brief. Soon they were able to move back to Newgate Street where they obtained a house of their own. This was near a small beerhouse originally called the "Railway Office" and later the "Major Oak" and which, together with its neighbouring cottages, has been long demolished. While living there, tragedy struck as, in 1855, Mr. Ward was killed in an accident at Shireoaks colliery, where he was then working. William, at sixteen, thus became the breadwinner for the family. Not that this would daunt him for he had been used to long hours of toil from his earliest years. He was only seven when he earned his first few pence bird tenting at Hawks' Nest farm, solitary work for so young a boy but by no means unusual in a household where every copper counted. Schooling was an occupation that few from poor families could afford or, indeed, saw the need of and William's time at the desk was very short. When he was about eleven [1] he did manage a few weeks at the Abbey Boys' School which then met in the gatehouse of the Priory Church. That brief interlude over, he returned to the land before following many other local youths to Shireoaks colliery, in search of a few extra shillings a week. For a while he worked in the boiler room before moving to Whalley near Manchester where he operated a portable steam engine.

Obviously this sort of work with its constant noise and oppressive atmosphere didn't suit him and he soon left the confines of the factory for the comparative freedom of the

William Ward was a member of the United Methodist Free Church which stood on Potter Street and was known as the Ebenezer Chapel. The original chapel of 1830 was replaced in 1875 and this is the interior that he would be familiar with from that year. As a local preacher he would, from time to time, occupy the pulpit though his appointments would more often be in the smaller outlying chapels of the circuit.

farm. He returned to Worksop and it was while he was working at Darfoulds that an incident occurred that changed the course of his life. One day, while he and another man were mowing, a party of gypsies paused on the nearby roadside. They had a donkey and cart with them and William Ward announced to his surprised companion that he thought that he would buy them. Laying down his scythe he walked across to the gypsies and, after a spell of intense haggling, became the owner, not only of the donkey and cart but also of the donkey's foal. Not having an immediate need for the latter, William sold it to a Mr. Drury of Shireoaks who gave it to the local postman, widely known as "Bacca" Jack and who was lame. With his new means of mobility, he was able to deliver the mail to Shireoaks, Thorpe Salvin and district for many years.

Meanwhile, William Ward set up as a higgler, buying coal from Shireoaks colliery, leading it to Worksop and selling it about the town. After a while he changed his wares from coal to pots and began the occupation that he was to follow for over forty years. It was his boast that he had hawked his pots in every village within a forty mile radius of Worksop. Indeed, he must have travelled further as, on occasions, he ventured as far as Hull, Manchester, Peterborough and Melton Mowbray. Such wanderings meant hard work for his donkeys and horses and he once stated that, over the years, he had owned over a hundred. How many pairs of boots he wore out over the same period is not known. That he spent so much time on his feet was all the more remarkable as, for many years, he suffered from a deformity of the legs. Just what that was and what caused it is not clear. As a youth and a young man he was perfectly fit; in fact he was well known locally as a prize fighter, on one occasion beating the "Retford Terror," a pugilist who was widely famed in his day. Whether his later difficulties were a result of his time in the ring or the rigours of his work or, indeed, a combination of both will now never be known. Certainly, the latter was not free of hazard. Once, while on Whitwell Hill, his horse bolted. Mr. Ward was thrown from his dray which ran over his legs, No bones were broken though he had to hobble on crutches for several weeks afterwards. This was not a solitary accident though others were not so serious. Such incidents no doubt contributed to his lameness and gave rise to his nick-name of "Peg-Leg" Ward.

In his early twenties, William Ward married a young woman from Northamptonshire. The ceremony took place at the Priory Church. His wife bore no fewer than seventeen children though only two, a boy and a girl, survived to their parents' old age. Mrs. Ward died in 1910. By then her husband was in his early seventies, shortly to sell his last horse and cart and retire from the trade that he had followed for so many years. Not that retirement brought idleness. Mr. Ward had been long associated with the Methodist chapel on Potter Street, fondly known as the Ebenezer chapel though more correctly the United Methodist Free Church, and was fully involved in its activities. His conversion brought about changes in his way of life. He gave up prize fighting, smoking and drinking and, instead, took up hymn singing, mission work and preaching. With others as a mission band and on his own as a local preacher he conducted services throughout the circuit where his "rugged but fervent oratory" found favour with the local congregations. Want of a musician didn't daunt him at the small, rural chapels for he had a good voice and could lead the hymn singing unaccompanied if necessary. He was also a talented whistler and while no doubt he beguiled the miles and attracted custom with this gift, it is perhaps unlikely that he used it during Sunday services.

Though born in near poverty, William Ward possessed a great spirit. He worked hard for every shilling that he earned, he overcame difficulties that would have disheartened lesser men and he tried to serve his fellow townspeople as fully as his abilities allowed. At his death, the town lost one of its great characters, a man who was known on every one of its streets and of whom it should have felt truly proud.

Notes and References

1. He is classified as a scholar in the 1851 census returns.

Shops and Shopping.

Throughout the 19th century, almost without exception, Worksop's shops were privately owned, the majority by people living within the town itself. In the early years they catered for the basic needs of their local customers though as the century progressed an occasional shop offering non-essential wares made its appearance. Shops varied in size from the commodious to the tiny, from those with extensive premises on the main thoroughfares to those that were no more than a room in a back street cottage. Apart from providing the town's necessities, the shops were also a valuable source of employment. In 1841 over two hundred and fifty people either owned or worked in them, the unmarried staff of some of the larger establishments living in with the proprietors. Thus, at the end of a long day making up orders or serving behind the counter, the two apprentices of Mr. Francis Hooson, grocer on the corner of Bridge Street with Potter Street, simply climbed the stairs to their attic bedroom above the shop.

Clothing, food and household necessities just about summarises the range of goods on offer in the early years of the century. The only additions to this essentially utilitarian list, as recorded in a local directory, were two booksellers and printers and four druggists.[1] Boot and shoemakers were in the majority. In 1832 there were at least twenty five of them[2] and this number remained fairly constant throughout the century. At its end, in 1900, there were still twenty two in business.[3] This seemingly large number is easily explained. At that time most of the townspeople were a walking population. Just a few kept a horse or a horse and trap, the rest had to get about on foot, creating a heavy demand for boots and shoes. For the greater part of the century these were hand made by local craftsmen though, by the 1880's, the beginnings of change were apparent. Nine described themselves as just shoemakers, giving the impression that they produced more fashionable wares and perhaps inferring that the town's streets were more suitable for lighter footwear than they had been earlier in the century. Factory made products were also appearing in some of the shops. By 1885 two men calling themselves boot factors were in business, their title suggesting that they sold ready mades rather than the products of their own workshops.

Just as local craftsman shod most feet in the town, so local tailors, dressmakers and milliners satisfied the demand for clothes and hats. There was always plenty of choice. Of the former, gentlemen could choose from eighteen in 1832. This number had risen to over twenty in mid-century but had fallen to ten by its end. For the ladies, there were fourteen milliners and dressmakers in 1832 and, although the number varied in the intervening years, it was the same in 1900. These figures, and those that follow, are taken from trade directories and should not be regarded as fully accurate. They give a good general idea of how many shops of each sort there were but tend to group together the small back street outlets and simply classify their owners as shopkeepers.

Among the twenty three in 1832 would surely be the odd jobbing tailor and the widow skilful with her needle who would eke out her days undertaking small tasks for her neighbours.

Not surprisingly, grocers and butchers formed the majority of the food shops though the numbers of each might seem rather excessive for the population of the time. In 1832 there were fourteen of the former and eighteen of the latter while by the end of the century the numbers had risen to thirty four and thirty seven respectively. As with the clothes' shops, many of these were small, of limited stock, perhaps of dubious quality and standards of hygiene. Very few of the early grocers' shops compared with that of Mr. John Eddison who, when his stock of fine tea, spices and similar special items was becoming depleted, mounted his horse and rode to London to order the necessary replenishments.[4] Likewise few, if any, of the butchers' shops of the end of the century could rival that of Mr. David Winks that stood on the Market Place and where only meat of prime quality was offered for sale. Few of the smaller shops could make such a boast. This was particularly so when animals were slaughtered in the shop itself. When, in 1858, the inspector of Nuisances checked all the slaughter houses in the town, he was especially concerned with the conditions at Mr. Foottit's where the work was carried out in the shop, blood seeping through the doorway and onto the pavement.

Food and clothing apart, in the early years of the century the provision of other goods was limited. There were four druggists in 1832 – a name to be replaced within twenty years by the now familiar one of chemist - four ironmongers, fourteen drapers of various sorts and five watch and clock makers. One noticeable omission was any shop dealing specifically with furniture though as three chair makers[5] were already in business that article, at least, ought to have been reasonably available. No doubt the four cabinet makers and four joiners supplied some of the other items. Thirty or more years were to pass before two furniture brokers were recorded in a local directory.[6]

Slowly the range of shops widened, some of the new business ventures offering goods of a less essential nature. By 1844[7] there were four confectioners, three nursery and seedsmen and two smallware dealers while ten years later [8]two shops dealt in glassware and similar items. Prior to 1869 it seems strange that no greengrocers and fruiterers are mentioned though probably some of those simply classified as shopkeepers provided such goods. However, in that year, two shops specifically selling fruit and vegetables were in business. At the same time several other shops offering new lines of goods sought the custom of local people. There were four earthenware dealers, a tobacconist, a haberdasher, a toy dealer who was also a barber and a newsagent. All these items must have been available before from shops selling other goods as well but there were also businesses that were new to the town. Two were photographers, one combining picture framing with his work behind the camera,. Nothing is known of them though Mrs. Emma Exley, who lived on the New Road (Newcastle Avenue) was presumably a widow. None of their photographs appear to have survived but what a discovery it would be if some did come to light: a gallery of worthies of mid-Victorian Worksop whose likenesses were hitherto unknown. During this time, a new name was applied to some shops, perhaps in an attempt to make them more attractive to potential customers. Two were called fancy repositories, places where little decorative extras could be bought, though that of Miss Charlotte Gibson was also an agency for the British and Foreign Bible Society.

Shops of this sort rarely lasted long. Mentioned in one directory, it was unusual for them to be included in the next. This was not so with another shop that opened in the 1860's. Its beginnings were modest, its eventual growth considerable and it is still in business today. The story begins in the Golden Ball where, sometime in 1866, a group of men met in earnest discussion. After a while, one of them, Mr. Sam. Hammond, took a half a crown (12.5p) from his pocket and put it on the table. "There, that will start the Worksop Co-operative Society," he said. Others present followed his example and at the end of the evening the amount that had been subscribed was handed over to the safe keeping of Mrs. Johnson, the landlady. Little by little the sum grew and when it reached £20 it was decided to open a shop. At the same time a set of rules was drawn up and agreed at a general meeting that was held on the 22nd. December, 1866. These were approved by the Registrar of Friendly Societies on the 21st. February of the following year. All the founders of the society were manual workers. Most of them, including Samuel Hammond, the first secretary, worked at Shireoaks colliery. One was a chair maker, another a butcher. All were family men in their thirties. It was in the home of another such man that the first shop was established. Edwin Crossley was a thirty eight year old wood turner who lived in a small cottage down Canal Road and it was one of its rooms that was fitted out as the shop. At first it only opened on two or three days a week and then only for a few hours. Whatever payment Edwin Crossley might have received did not constitute a living wage and four years after the opening he was still described as a wood turner and grocer.[9] Sometime later, following differences with the committee, he resigned and the society faced its first major crisis. A meeting to decide its future was held at the Waterford Inn which stood at the junction of Sandy Lane with Gateford Road. Twelve members attended and when the vital vote was taken whether to remain open or to close, support was equal. Everything depended on the casting vote of the chairman and he opted to continue in business. For a while this took place from a house in Bridge Place, before moving a little later to 11, Eastgate. This proved to be a street especially favoured by the society and from that time until its closure in 2000 its central premises have been situated on it.

With the coming of the Co-operative Society, a new idea of business was introduced to the town. In every other shop the profits were retained by the owner: at the Co-op, they were shared between the members in proportion to the amount that they had spent. This was the dividend, or divi. as it was generally known; a painless way of saving and a boon to many families where every penny counted. Some still alive will remember the crowd that gathered outside the Co-op. offices early on "divi day," people eager to receive their share of the society's profits, however small it might be. Few details have survived of early trading but it is known that in the second half of 1869 sales totalled £720 which, with all expenses paid, left a balance of £36 - 2 - 1d. (£36-10.5p). Other grocers in the town would ruefully shake their heads when they learnt of these figures, regretting the loss of such amounts from their tills. Whatever animosity might have existed between local shopkeepers and the new movement, for many people it was a blessing and, after early teething problems, it became firmly established in the town.[10]

At the same time that the Co-op. was struggling into existence, another firm with a name soon to be widely known was inviting local custom. This was W.H. Smith and by 1872 they had a bookstall on the railway station. Thus the business man could beguile the miles to his Sheffield office as he read the morning paper. Of more interest to the housewife was a new product offered by Mr. W. Middleton at his draper's shop on Bridge Street. As well as his usual products, he was also an agent for sewing machines. For those who could afford them, tedious hours with the needle were considerably reduced.

Ten years later another invention of the time was available in the town. In 1885 Mr. Tom. Castle whose coach building workshop was at 16, Gateford Road, soon to be known as Victoria Square,[11] was recorded as being an agent and dealer for bicycles and tricycles.[12] The impact of the bicycle in Worksop was considerable. Once acquired it gave its owner a hitherto undreamt of means of mobility. It reduced the travelling time to and from work, it opened up the surrounding countryside, it introduced new events to sports meetings and, unlike the horse, maintenance costs were negligible. Within a few years Worksop had its cycle makers as well as agents. Best known was Mr. George Vardy who, by 1891, was established in business in Bridge Place. Six years later he moved to purpose built premises on Ryton Street where twenty machines of his own "Dukeries" model were made each week.

The three brass balls prominently fixed to the front of Patterson and Son's Potter Street premises indicate that it was a pawn shop. Here people in financial need could deposit articles of clothing, household goods, watches and the like in return for a temporary loan. If the articles were not redeemed within a set period, they could be sold. This building still stands though it is no longer a shop.

Early bicycles were not cheap. The purchase of a new one was beyond the pockets of many of the poor people of the town. They were more likely to patronise another shop that was first recorded at the same time that bicycles were appearing on the streets. This was the pawn shop and by 1885 Mr. John Patterson and Mrs. Sarah Patterson were proprietors of two such establishments, one on Potter Street and the other on Gateford Road. Here those who couldn't make ends meet deposited articles of clothing, pieces of furniture, watches, jewellery and the like in return for a small temporary cash loan, to be repaid, plus interest, within a specified time. Failure to redeem the pledges meant that they would be forfeited and would probably appear for sale in the pawnbroker's window shortly afterwards. It seems rather strange that such shops were not listed as being in town until the 1890's. They were certainly in business in other places before then. Perhaps, in Worksop, the owners preferred to be classified in the directories as just shopkeepers. Pawnbroking was not a prestigious occupation and even the Pattersons tried to soften the implicit harshness of their calling by styling themselves as pawnbrokers and clothiers, though the garments that they offered for sale had usually been deposited as security for loans and never redeemed.

By the end of the nineteenth century a new type of shop was beginning to appear on Worksop's streets. This was a branch store of a company that was based out of town and may also have had similar outposts in a number of other places as well. The first of these stores to make a real impact in the town was the grandly named Cosmopolitan Provision Stores. It occupied fine premises in the recently completed Dallas Yorke Buildings on Bridge Place and thither, no doubt to the consternation of the local grocers, people flocked in their hundreds. One who remembered those days wrote of them much later in his life, "Its success was immediate, and within a matter of days satisfied customers were persuading their neighbours and friends of savings to be effected by obtaining their necessities at the new shop."[13] It is doubtful if the owners of the new shop spent much, if any, time in it, the customers would be welcomed by Mr. Samuel J. Rice, the manager. This was to be a position that was to become increasingly numerous as the new century progressed and the multiples made further inroads into the town. Where the Cosmopolitan led, others followed, though, perhaps, with less threat to existing businesses. Brailsford and Company, Tobacconist and Cigar Manufacturer, a Sheffield based firm, could hardly be regarded as serious competitors to the four shops already trading in those wares. Customers were simply given a wider choice. This was also true when the Midland Boot Company opened a branch at 48 Bridge Street. The situation was a little different when Clark and Company, dyers, cleaners and steam laundry men, offered to take some of the toil out of the weekly wash day though here the only people who might regret their coming were the handful of women who earned a few coppers tackling the washing from some of the better off homes.

Whatever the thoughts of the shopkeepers and the townspeople in general on the coming of the multiples, the recently established Worksop Guardian was in no two minds on the subject. It saw no benefit at all in them and strongly advocated support for the local shopkeepers. It pointed out the advantages of trading with someone who was known, who would employ fellow townspeople and, "has no interest in pushing low quality American provisions under English names." The, "value and variety," of the locally owned shop, "is apparent, relevant and reliable," it added and continued to make its final and fundamental point that, "the money you spend each week with your townsman is not sent out of the town, but kept in circulation to benefit all."[14] Few reading these words in the summer of 1897 would take them too seriously. With less multiples and branch shops in town than could be counted on the fingers of one hand, they posed no danger. As their number increased, the foresight of the writer in the Guardian became more apparent.

One other type of shop which opened for business in the final years of the 19th century found immediate favour and still thrives though its fare nowadays is somewhat wider. This was the fried fish shop. By 1900 there were two in business, one of them, that of Mr. George England, prominently situated on Bridge Place. It is perhaps a happy thought to conclude this survey of Worksop's shops of the nineteenth century with this picture of an innovative, successful and still local venture. There were others, of course, who thought that they could fill a gap in the local market. Some, like Mr. England, succeeded, others didn't. Little more was heard of the muffin baker of 1900 or the tea and butter man of the same year. They obviously couldn't provide either a better or a cheaper product than the bakers or the grocers and so they failed

Over the century shops had increased in number to cater for the ever growing population, they had widened the variety of goods on offer, reflecting the availability of new household goods and the ability of more people to afford what might be called luxury rather than purely functional items. Few, if any, shopkeepers, however, would have reviewed their prospects rosily. Fluctuations in trade could put hundreds out of work, if only temporarily, and reduce the spending potential of the town overnight. Industrial disputes in the coal industry had the same effect. Memories lingered of the miners' lockout of 1893 when the local pits were closed for sixteen weeks. Little on the shelves and less in the till were common experiences of those hard times. If the past recalled such days then the future was not without its fears. Rumblings of these were already apparent and have been mentioned. One was the continued, steady growth of the Co-operative Society. By the end of the century, it had added drapery, millinery and furnishing departments to its central premises on Eastgate as well as opening a branch on Lowtown Street together with another and a bakery on Newcastle Avenue. But perhaps its greatest challenge to local businessmen came in 1904 when it opened premises on Watson Road. These housed several departments - drapery, household furnishings, ladies' outfitting and the like - under the same roof and was rather grandly known as an emporium. Worksop had never seen such a shop. The Society had certainly progressed since its early days in the tiny room of the Canal Road cottage.

A second possible source of concern was the potential threat of the multiple firms. The Cosmopolitan Provision stores was followed by the Globe Tea Company and the Midland

This photograph was taken in 1886 and is the oldest in the book. It shows a group of shops at the top end of Potter Street, just below Hooson's which is illustrated on a later picture. There were several dual-purpose shops in second half of the 19th century Worksop though the combination of barber and umbrella repairer must be the most unusual. White's, next door was a milliner's and dressmakers. (Photograph by permission of the Bassetlaw Museum).

Dairy Company[15] and although they enjoyed a fair share of trade, few shopkeepers at first saw their livelihoods at risk from such incursions. This situation changed as the new century progressed: slowly at first, but gradually developing such a momentum that it has now almost, but not quite, driven the private shop from the main streets. Here and there, hemmed in by multiple and supermarket, by building society and charity shop, the occasional survivor still stands, often a shop of quality, sometimes one of many years trading. Long may they continue.

Neither longevity nor attractiveness were qualities that applied to many shops in 19th century Worksop, but to some they certainly did. Many were ordinary in appearance and humdrum in stock but some stood out from their neighbours in one way or another. Two had just been there a long time. They had been in business before most of their customers were born and were still trading after most of them had died. One was the shop of the Sissons family who were principally booksellers, printers and stationers though their interests were much wider and included, at different times, patent medicines, pianofortes, paperhanging, a newsagency and a circulating library. Towards the end of the 19th century their display of guidebooks, postcards and souvenirs of the Dukeries were especially popular with visitors. Their shop stood prominently at the top of Potter Street, a seemingly immovable landmark in the town. It now forms part of the Civic Centre complex. Exactly when the business was founded will perhaps never be known, though the late Mr. Vincent Sissons had a letter head dated within the second half of the 18th century.[16] Perhaps the firm's greatest achievement was the successful launching of the Worksop Guardian in 1896.

Contemporary with Sissons was the firm of Reuben Shaw and Son, ironmongers. As with Sissons, their interests were much wider than can be summarised in one word. In 1872 they were described as furnishing and general ironmongers, whitesmiths, bellhangers and glass and china dealers. With so many departments, it is not surprising that Shaws was one of the largest firms in the town. In 1861 its work force totalled twenty, including two apprentices.[17] Not all of these served behind the counters, for some were craftsmen who either spent their time in a workshop at the back of the main premises or carried out commissions in the town and district. Such a man was Mr. Edward Bell who worked for Shaws for forty two years as a whitesmith and bell hanger.

Known throughout the 19th century as Hooson's Corner, the junction of Potter Street with Bridge Street was named after the shop that stood there. For the best part of a hundred years it was owned by successive members of the Hooson family, beginning with Francis Hooson in the early years of the century. Though primarily a grocer's, the range of goods on sale was much wider than such shops usually offered. When this photograph was taken around 1906, the shop had been taken over by Mr. A.H. James. (Photograph by permission of the Bassetlaw Museum).

In the former capacity he made and fitted dozens of smoke jacks, a device patented by Shaws and which, for a number of years, was widely installed in larger properties. On one occasion Mr. Bell had to travel as far as Scarborough to fit one in the Grand Hotel. While smithing was his everyday task, bell hanging was his speciality and his particular pride was the work that he did at Welbeck Abbey where he is said to have, "hung many miles of bell wire.[18]

Shaws was one of the back-bone shops of the town. Like Sissons it had a re-assuring permanence and within its range of stock it was able to supply every want. China, glass and earthenware, stoves, chimney pieces, fire irons, brass and iron bedsteads, gas lamps and fittings of all kinds, cutlery: all these, in addition to general items of ironmongery, were always available. No wonder that the shop at 13. Bridge Street enjoyed popular patronage: no wonder that, "Go to Shaws," was an oft-given recommendation.

Like Francis Sissons, Reuben Shaw set up in business in the second half of the eighteenth century. The exact year may never be known though when Mr. Henry Shaw died in 1863 his obituary notice stated that the firm of which he had been a managing partner, "extends back fully for 125 years."[19] This would set the year of its foundation as 1738 though, as the evidence for this is not too positive, it would perhaps be wise to regard the date as approximate. What is certain is that both Shaws and Sissons opened their doors to the people of Worksop for over two hundred years and it was not until the changing economic times of the 1960's that those doors were closed for the last time.

Other shops, though not as long lasting, in their day enjoyed the custom of the townspeople as well as adding a touch of originality, even novelty to the main streets. One of the most noticeable was than of Hooson Brothers. They were grocers and their shop stood opposite the market on what was widely known as Hooson's corner. Mr. Francis Hooson, generally referred to as "Old Franky," opened for business in the early years of the 19th century and, passing first to a nephew, also Francis, and then to succeeding generations of the family continued to trade for about a hundred years. In 1866 the firm extended its commercial interests when it bought the Park Brewery at Sheffield and, shortly afterwards, in 1870 it had its own maltings built on Eastgate. These varied activities were all reflected in the shop as, painted on its frontage, was a catalogue of its wares. "Hooson Bros" it read, "maltsters, brewers, hop merchants, provision dealers, wines, fruits and dealers in British and foreign cigars." And if that wasn't enough, they were also bakers. As with many shops of the time, Hoosons displayed as many goods outside the premises as the width of the pavement and local bye-laws permitted. One whose memory went back to the latter

Hardly Worksop's most impressive shops and yet the one on the extreme left was one of the most popular. It was owned by Mrs. Elizabeth (Sally) Bramer who sold home made sweets. At Christmas time, so it was said, tins of them were sent to Worksop people who had emigrated to the four corners of the world. Long ago, the whole block, which stood on Bridge Street, also contained a fruiterer's shop, a barber's and an earthenware dealer's. (Photograph by permission of Mr. H. Lamb).

years of the 19th century recalled seeing a, "massive display of cheese on the pavement underneath the Bridge Street shop window flanked by two gigantic pockets of hops at each side of the doorway.[20] Shopping at Hooson's must have been quite an experience. The building itself was one of the oldest in the town dating to the 17th century or even earlier, its original timber framework hidden from view by subsequent layers of plaster. With such a variety of goods on open view, within the limited confines of the shop, the prevailing aroma must have been one not speedily forgotten.

The neighbouring shop on Bridge Street was a little unusual too. Quite early in the century, Mr. Tom. Marris set up as a druggist there. Not one for having all his eggs in one basket, he was also the proprietor of an ironmonger's shop that stood almost opposite on Bridge Street and owned a small foundry on Potter Street. However, it was the chemist's shop that was of particular interest for along with pills, potions and medicines, Mr. Marris also sold wines and spirits. It was his son Tom, though, who introduced a feature to the business that some would claim made it unique. He opened a small bar at the back of the shop. Thus, his customers, if they so wished, could wash away the unpleasant taste of their medicine with a glass of something more acceptable to the palate. There is no doubt that the Marris's dual business thrived and that the little bar proved a popular rendezvous with the townspeople. In 1874 Mr. Tom Marris produced the first issue of his Almanack. This was to appear annually until the outbreak of World War 1. Although it did contain a calendar, some useful information and general reading matter, it was primarily a means of advertising the fare on offer in the shop. Its range, both of wines and spirits, and medicaments was extensive, the latter consisting of standard proprietary products and "home made" remedies. Of these Marris's Universal Cough Balsam was the most widely celebrated. Mr. Marris boasted its efficacy in the Almanack, "It is undoubtedly the best remedy known for Coughs, Colds, Asthma, Bronchitis, Hoarseness, Difficulty of breathing, and all Affections of the Throat and Lungs." Relief from such afflictions could be obtained for 1s, (5p) or 2s. 6d. (12-1/2p) a bottle. Apparently its main ingredient was black treacle.

Perhaps the most eye-catching shop in the town stood a little further along Bridge Street. It was another dual purpose establishment and, until his death in 1885, its proprietor was Mr. Job Ebenezer Cartledge, a noted eccentric whose great

Although by 1907 this shop on the Bridge Place Watson Road corner was owned by G.T. Smith, it was still widely remembered as Leonard Towne's. He came to Worksop in the 1860's and set up as a grocer on Bridge Street, later moving to the premises shown on this picture. A selection of his goods was always most attractively displayed in the windows and often, especially on the days before Christmas, people would pause to gaze even if they couldn't afford to buy.

ambition was to represent Bassetlaw in Parliament. His actual occupation was less exalted for he was a barber though doubtless he was never loath to express his political opinions to his clients as he plied his scissors and razor. His second occupation, however, attracted far younger customers to his window than those who sat in his chair for he was also a toy seller. In 1869, when he was first recorded as such,[21] he was the only one in the town, though probably would not enjoy much custom. Money was too tight in many households to permit spending on such items and most children had to be content with gazing into his window and wishing. It was when his shop was closed that it stood out from its neighbours at its stock was secured for the night behind "patchwork shutters." Across the road and further up Bridge Street, in an old, low building long since demolished was a shop which was equally popular with both young and old. This was where Mrs. Elizabeth Bramer - better known as Sally, sold her home made sweets. Greatest favourites were her bulls' eyes and butter scotch but she had other varieties on offer as well. It is said that Worksop people living in other parts of the country would always take away a good supply of Sally's sweets when returning from a visit to their hometown and that parcels of them were shipped world wide to local families who had either emigrated or were working overseas.[22]

If these last two shops represented the more unusual ones in the town, then those of Mr. Leonard Towne and Mr. David Winks can be taken as examples of the more orthodox, and of the highest quality too. The former was a grocer, the latter a butcher and both were in business throughout the last decades of the century. Leonard Towne came from Retford in 1863 and soon established a grocery business on Bridge Street. Later he had new premises built on the corner of Bridge Place with Watson Road and traded from there until his retirement. His was not the sort of shop that anyone would go into for a pennyworth of sugar. Ladies would expect to be shown to a chair and to be served, if not by Mr. Towne himself, then by a counter hand who had completed a long apprenticeship in the trade. All but the smallest requirements were carefully listed and delivered to the customer's home. Window dressing was a skill widely practiced in the town and the displays in Mr. Towne's shop were particularly noted, especially at Christmas time. Those whose meagre purse deterred them from entering could gain some envious pleasure from gazing at the fare so temptingly set out for all to see.

Mr. Winks' shop was at the opposite end of the town, on the Market Place, almost facing the Old Ship Inn. He was a Worksop man, as proud of his local connections as he was of the quality of the meat that he offered for sale. When applicable, he liked to boast that this was from animals that were reared on the estates of the Dukeries. Prime joints rather than scrag end were David Winks' stock in trade and the customers who entered his shop reflected that. Today he is perhaps better remembered as the grandfather of William and Walter Straw than as the town's principal butcher.

These are but a small selection of Worksop's shops of the 19th century. They would be known to everyone in the town either for their seeming permanence, or their individual character, or the excellence of their wares. The reputation of few, if any, of them, however, extended to the neighbouring towns and beyond. There was one shop, though, that could claim that distinction. This was the Park Street bookshop of Robert White, by repute even patronized by the Queen. As it is described elsewhere[23] it is sufficient to repeat that it was a shop unique in the commercial history of the town. By the end of the 19th century, Worksop seemed to be well served by its shops. Their number had increased to keep pace with the growing population and the variety of goods they offered had widened to cater for changing tastes and greater prosperity. Some of the shops had been trading for so long that they were almost regarded as institutions. These and some established more recently were to continue in business well into the 20th century. Others were less permanent. Opened in optimism, they survived for awhile before putting up their shutters for the last time. As for the shopkeepers, most of those whose businesses were going concerns looked to the future with some confidence. They had coped with the competition from the Co-operative Society, whilst the threat from the multiples seemed too remote to be of immediate danger. If they sought assurance for the future, the sight of Mr. William Straw walking from his grocer's shop on the Market Place to the bank, his daily takings, rumoured largely to be in sovereigns. in a bucket, might well provide that.

Notes and References

1. W. White. Directory of Nottinghamshire. 1832.

2. Ibid.

3. Kelly's Directory of Nottinghamshire. 1900

4. M.J. Jackson. Victorian Worksop. 1992

5. W. White. Directory of Nottinghamshire. 1852.

6. Morris and Co. Commercial Directory And Gazetteer of Nottinghamshire. 1869.

7. W. White. Directory of Nottinghamshire, 1844.

8. Ibid. 1853.

9. 1871 Census Returns.

10. The Centenary brochure of the Worksop Co-operative Society and the Worksop Guardian, 20 February, 1970.

11. The name was introduced following the Golden Jubilee of Queen Victoria in 1887. The area was previously known as the Common End.

12. W. White. Directory of Nottinghamshire, 1885-86.

13. "The March of the Multiple Stores," an undated cutting from the Worksop Guardian, probably c.1970. Although published anonymously, the writer could have been the late Mr. Edwin Topham.

14. The Worksop Guardian, 11 June, 1897.

15. Ibid.

16. Mr. Sissons showed the writer this piece of ephemera who, unfortunately, did not note its date at the time.

17. Census Returns, 1861.

18. The Worksop Guardian, 4 March, 1904.

19. The Retford and Gainsborough Times, 31 August, 1883.

20. An undated cutting from the Worksop Guardian of an article by Wanderer.

21. Morris and Co. Commercial Directory and Gazetteer of Nottinghamshire, 1869.

22. An undated article in the Worksop Guardian by Edwin Topham.

23 See "Bookseller to the Queen," pages 81-86

Worksop's Bible Woman.

Many stricken with illness or incapacitated by accident in mid-Victorian Worksop had to suffer at home, often untended by skilled medical attention. This was widely so with those too poor to pay for a visit from one of the half dozen or so doctors in practice in the town. There was no hospital though a dispensary which opened in 1867 provided some relief for those eligible to receive it. This was entirely medicinal in its nature; it had no facilities to offer any residential care. Only the infirmary of the Union Workhouse could provide that though few would seek it unless driven there by desperation and hopelessness. The occupants of many a sick bed had to face endless hours of loneliness, pain and discomfort, unvisited and uncared for.

One who was aware of this situation and determined to do something about it was Mrs. Fanny Stenton. Biographical details are scarce and the most that can be stated with any certainty is that she was the wife of John Stenton who was a chairmaker and lived on Eastgate. According to the 1861 census he was 54, his wife two years older. At home with them were two sons, both chairmakers, a daughter and a four year old grand-daughter who could have been the child of their daughter Eliza, mentioned in the 1851 census but unrecorded ten years later. At that earlier date Fanny Stenton was classified as a grocer which could have meant no more than having a little shop in one

This could almost be a drawing of Fanny Stenton going about her mission of bringing comfort, company and readings from the Bible to the sick and housebound people of the town. It isn't, of course, but it does give a good idea of a part of the town, unrecognisable to the present eye, with which she would have been familiar. Not one of these buildings on Bridge Place of the 1860's is still in being. The tall chimney was part of Mapson's mill which stood on the canal side. (Picture from the Cecil Brown collection at Worksop Library).

Duck Row, a bit of Westgate, as this picture is captioned, was one of the poorest parts of the town and was mentioned by Fanny Stenton in her diary. It is said to have been given its unusual name as people of normal height had to duck their heads when going through the front doors. (Picture by permission of Mr. H. Lamb.)

of the rooms of her home. Even when all their sources of income were added together they would provide but modest means for the family's subsistence. However, out of whatever small surplus there might have been, between August, 1864 and November, 1865 Mrs. Stenton took a few coppers and bought two slim exercise books. Using them as diaries, she chronicled her ministrations to the poor, heading the first of them, "Journal of Fanny Stenton, Bible Woman."[1] They tell, albeit in the briefest outline, a remarkable story of one woman's determination to bring a little comfort and caring to those in the greatest need.

Such people invariably lived in the poorer parts of the town and Fanny Stenton's journal is dotted with the names of back streets, courts and yards unmarked on street plans and untrodden by most townspeople. Malt Kiln Row, Bowle's Yard, Duck Row, Forrest's Yard, Bedlam Square and Davis' Row were some of these insalubrious byways. Usually, on her visits, she simply sat with the ailing person, read to them from the Bible and said a prayer. Sometimes, however, she was able to dispense material as well as spiritual comfort. From time to time well-wishers gave her useful articles and small sums of money to help her in her work. These she immediately used to full advantage. Thus Selena Burbridge who was, "very poorly of rheumatic fever," was given a pair of sheets and pillow cases, items not too common in the poorest homes, but which would make the sick bed a little more comfortable. Similarly, Mrs. Coupe was given a bottle of wine and another woman, a shilling (5p). Mrs. Stenton didn't discriminate. If a person was needy, sick and lonely then that person would be visited. It didn't matter that Mary

Ann was a woman, "who bears a bad character." She was very ill and so she was called upon several times. On one occasion, as well as reading to her and praying for her, Mrs. Stenton also took some vinegar to bathe her head.

From the 1840's the Marecroft area was filled with terraces of small, cramped cottages: cheaply built of brick and lacking most necessary facilities. It was a place where disease was endemic and a part of the town regularly visited by Fanny Stenton. This photograph was taken just before the property was demolished, the tiny gardens long abandoned, the outlook bleak and depressing.

No personal details are recorded in the diaries. Mrs. Stenton doesn't mention either home, family or any other aspect of her life. Not that she appeared to have much time for anything more than her visiting. This pattern was broken each week on Sunday. Not once did she make an entry for that day. No doubt she attended services at either the town's Priory church or one of the non-conformist chapels but she gave no indication which that was. Perhaps, too, and this may be fanciful thinking, she found time for a restful hour, seated on one of the Windsor chairs made by her husband in his daily work.

However she may have spent her Sundays, the time soon passed and each Monday brought about a renewal of her week day visiting. This, she varied from time to time by arranging meetings that several people who were ailing but not bed ridden could attend. Thus, at the close of Wednesday, the 10th August, 1864 she wrote, "Had a meeting in the afternoon at Ann Hancock's in Kilton Road, read the 8th chapter of the Acts of the Apostles." On another occasion, the 20th September, 1864 she recorded, "We had a very good meeting, the house was quite full," This pattern of meetings was broken on the 13th September, 1864 when, "Ann Keeling and 6 of us went to the Independent Chapel this afternoon instead of holding a meeting," The reason for this change is not given. Perhaps there was a special service on that day, certainly the venue was convenient. Standing on Westgate, the chapel was quite close to Lead Hill and several other areas of very poor housing where Mrs, Stenton was a regular visitor.

Ministering to the sick was not the only way in which she demonstrated her zeal for the bible. As well as reading from it, she also tried to make more copies available for others to use. When opportunity offered she helped to sell them as on the 12th October when she, "Stood with a stall of Bibles and Testaments, sold not quite as many as last time," She tried again a few weeks later on the 9th November when the town was crowded with farm workers and servants for the annual Statutes Fair, This was the day on which those who wanted to change their employment sought new situations and once that had been completed, the pursuit of entertainment and pleasure often ensued and money tended to burn a hole in pockets. Of all that was spent, just 9s, 9d (49p) was paid out for Mrs. Stenton's bibles and testaments. Whether she regarded this as a satisfactory day's business, she does not say, A little earlier, on the first of the month, she spent some time on a somewhat different errand of bible distribution. This involved a visit to one of the most disliked, even feared buildings in the town: the Union Workhouse. Before crossing its forbidding threshold she first collected thirteen testaments that had been bought by the girls who boarded at Miss Wilson's school on Cheapside. These she duly distributed to some of the poor children whose dismal young lives were spent under the frugal care of the Board of Guardians.

Virtually nothing is known of Mrs. Stenton's activities after November of 1865 when she completed the second of her surviving journals. That she continued her work is, at least, suggested by the appropriate entry in the 1871 census returns. By then she was 66 and a widow, living with her daughter Mary, her husband Benjamin Morton and their four infant children. Her new home was quite close to her old one, standing on the corner of Eastgate with George Street, part of the ground floor serving as a shop, as it does today. There Benjamin Morton supported his family as a draper and grocer. Whether his mother-in-law utilized her earlier experience in the latter line and assisted in the shop is not known though doubtless, as a caring grandmother, she would help her daughter with her young children. That she also found time for the avocation by which she was known throughout the town is more certain for against her name in the census return and in the column headed occupation are the two words "Bible Woman."

Notes and References

1. Both these books are now held in the Bassetlaw Museum.

Bookseller to the Queen.

One day in the early years of the last century, a young boy was walking with his father along Potter Street. Approaching them a lady was pushing a wicker sided bath chair. As they passed, the father, indicating its occupant, said to his son, "Take a good look at that man for he is one of the most remarkable in Worksop." The boy saw a frail, white whiskered old man wearing a wide brimmed straw hat. The father saw Robert White, antiquary, writer, master printer and bookseller to the Queen.[1]

Robert White was born on the 26th November, 1819 and died on the 1st November, 1908. He grew up the youngest child of the family with at least three brothers and a sister. His father died comparatively young, probably shortly after Robert's birth, and upon his mother, Mary White, devolved the responsibility of bringing up her family. From her home on Bridge Street she set up as a dressmaker and so continued until her children were able to look after themselves.

This would be a familiar sight for Robert White as he walked from his Park Place home to his book shop and printing works which were on Park Street. The man on the extreme right of the picture is standing close to the entry that led to his premises. By the time this photograph was taken, Robert White had retired though the printing business was still operating under his name.

Little is known of Robert's early years and nothing of his education. On leaving school he began working for a printer. There were at least two such businesses in Worksop at that time, the already well established firm of Sissons and that of John Whitlam. The address of the latter was Coney Street, a short stretch of road running southwards from the market into Park Street and a name soon to disappear from the town map. By 1848[2] Robert White had his own business in Coney Street and the likelihood is that he had taken over John Whitlam's works as his name was no longer being recorded in local trade directories. Whether Robert White had been originally apprenticed to John Whitlam and had, when circumstances favoured him, succeeded to his former master's business is not known but it is a happy thought that it might have been so. To have achieved this before his thirtieth birthday was no mean feat but it proved to be just one event among several that marked the late 1840's as an especially significant period in his life.

Set back from Park Street, Park Place is a hidden part of Worksop of which many passers-by are unaware. Robert White lived in the house on the left of the block. A keen antiquary, he obtained a marble statue that originally formed part of a frieze in the great temple at Pergamon in Asia Minor and which subsequently stood in the grounds of Worksop Manor. Robert White placed it against the gable wall of his house where it remained until the 1960's when it was donated to Worksop Museum.

As a young man he attended the Independent Chapel on Westgate[3] and on the 31st. January, 1845 he was admitted as a member. Whether his eyes strayed during the sermon or whether they were otherwise acquainted will never be known but two years later he married Miss Elizabeth Tyzack who was also a member of the church. She was the daughter of Joseph Tyzack, the principal of a private school on Park Street and before her marriage she had taught there. Sadly, the young couple's time together was short. Within two or three years Robert White experienced the joy of parenthood and the grief of bereavement. Elizabeth died shortly after giving birth to a daughter, Ann Tyzack White, and by 1851 Robert was living with his unmarried brother William at 20, Bridge Street. Ann, presumably, was being cared for by one of his relations, perhaps his sister.

At such a sad time it was fortunate that Robert White had much to occupy his days. As well as being a printer he was also a bookseller and had already developed an engrossing interest in the history and antiquities of his home town. In essence, his shop and printing works were Robert White's small world for the next fifty years. Apart from serving as clerk for a short time to the recently formed Local Board of Health, he showed little interest in civic affairs and although he provided the town with its first newspaper his name did not often feature in the columns of the local press. He was a private man, fully absorbed in building up his business, immersed in his study of the district's history and the preservation of its records.

Robert White's bookshop holds a unique place in Worksop's business history. There never before had been one like it: never since has it been equalled, nor, indeed, is it ever likely to be. Eventually he boasted a stock of over twenty thousand volumes, packed into every room of his Park Street

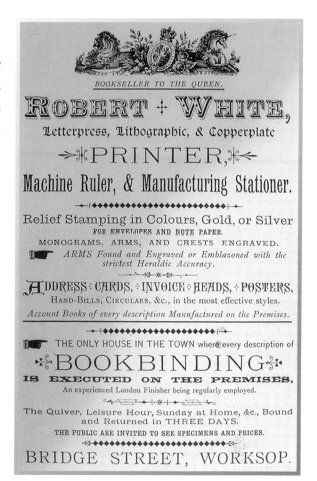

This advertisement appeared in Robert White's Household Almanack of 1886. It gives a good idea of some of the printing services that he could provide and, while not mentioning his book shop, it does state his claim to be "Bookseller to the Queen".

It would be interesting to know what transactions took place to justify such a title.

premises. The most attractive were usually set out in the shop itself but the most valuable and his own favourites rarely left his small office at the back of the building. A friend who knew that room, once described it. "Here were books from floor to ceiling," he wrote, "on the shelves, on the floor, and here there and everywhere; on his writing table where books only left a small margin for writing purposes and on his work table by the somewhat dim and dingy window."[4]

Robert White's shop enjoyed wide patronage, ranging from the indigent browser to the Queen herself. It would be fascinating to know details of the transaction that led to White styling himself 'Bookseller to the Queen' but, sadly, they are lost. Perhaps this aspect of Robert White's life can be best summarised in the words of one who knew him well, "As a book lover, a book knower and an old book seller he had no provincial equal."[5]

Equally widespread was his reputation as a printer. This was not based on the everyday output of his workshop, which consisted of the usual small town ephemera of posters, bills, leaflets, pamphlets, booklets and the like. This was the bread and butter work that he needed to enable him to undertake the production of high quality books, a much more satisfying though financially risky aspect of his trade. He began in a comparatively modest way. Two of the earliest books from his press were quite unexceptional. One, published in 1850, was "Discussion at Worksop", a verbatim report of a debate between an Anglican clergyman and a Catholic priest and another, of 1852, "Letters to Farmers" was based on a series of lectures given by James Hayward[6] to the Blyth Farmers' Club. It was with later publications that Robert White attracted the attention of the London reviewers. "The printing executed at Worksop, is equal to the best London work," stated The Bookseller while the Antiquary was similarly generous, ".. .. .. the typography, which we should imagine has never been equalled yet, and certainly never surpassed, in any book printed far away from the metropolis." Some of the books that helped him gain such a reputation were "Steetley Church" by James Cotencin, published in 1860, "The History of Roche Abbey," by James H. Aveling, 1870, and "Historic Notices of Rotherham" by John Guest, 1879. All three were opulently produced, issued only in limited editions and would demand extremely high prices if they were to come onto the market today.[7]

Three of his other printing ventures were of a quite innovative nature. The first of these was a local newspaper, The Worksop Journal, issued monthly. It first appeared in 1854 and continued for four or five years. It was a modest publication, consisting of a cover which contained local news, comments and advertisements and a bought in insert of more general interest. Its comparatively short life indicates that it wasn't generally popular. Much more so was Robert White's Household Almanack and Yearbook of Useful Knowledge. Early issues were quite slender booklets; later ones much more bulky. All were packed tight with local information, calendar notes, articles, quotations, "interesting gleanings and gatherings" and a galaxy of advertisements. At one penny (0.5p) a copy they were within the pocket of all and enjoyed a wide sale.

The third of Robert White's speculative products was a local guide, "The Visitors' Handbook to Worksop and its Neighbourhood," published in 1849. It was a handy little booklet of seventy two pages with sections on the Lords of the Manor of Worksop, the Priory, the appearance of the town, the Dukeries, Sherwood Forest and other places of interest in the district. Neatly illustrated with drawings by local artists, it sold for 6d. (2.5p) a copy. The year of its publication coincided with the coming of the railway to Worksop and the beginning of the flood of summer visitors to the town and district, a fact, no doubt, that Robert White had in mind while hastily compiling the first edition. Others followed at regular intervals. While working on the "Visitors' Handbook," White saw in his mind's eye a much more substantial volume, one treating the history of the town and district in far greater depth. He announced this hope in the second edition of the "Handbook" but twenty five years were to pass before it appeared.

"Worksop 'The Dukery' and Sherwood Forest" was published in 1875 in two editions.

One, at 7s 6d (37.5p) was neat and attractive: the other at £1 1s (£1.05) to subscribers and £1 10s 0d (£1.50) to others was a larger and more handsome volume. It was a book of over three hundred pages of which White wrote about half, his contribution being, in the main, an amplification of the text of the "Visitors' Handbook." The rest consisted of six articles by local contributors and a selection of extracts from writings on the Forest. It is generously illustrated and, after over a hundred and twenty years, is still quite an easy and worth-while read. On publication it was well received, one reviewer commenting, "A pleasant book about a pleasant place is always among the pleasantest of circumstances. Mr. White's book has further pleasant qualifications. He has written, compiled and edited it; and he is both the printer and publisher. We should not be surprised to hear that he has drawn all the charming illustrations."[8]

A present day reader would probably regret the lack of social and economic material and find the second part, the contributed articles, the most interesting. Robert White wouldn't have minded such a judgement of posterity for he was a reluctant author. Much as he wished to publish a history of Worksop, he hoped that someone else would write it. It was only when he felt that such a person was not forthcoming that he sorted his notes and began the work himself. Such was his modesty however, that his name was not printed on the title page. He was more of an antiquary than a historian. His particular interest and pleasure was in collecting, in gathering together material about Worksop and district. This is well illustrated in his final book.

For a number of years Robert White hoped to bring out a revised and extended edition of "Worksop 'The Dukery' and Sherwood Forest" but subscriptions towards the cost were disappointing and the idea was abandoned. Instead, when he was in his eighties, he arranged, edited and published an extensive selection from the antiquarian riches of his life time's store. This was "Dukery Records," a large volume of four hundred and twenty pages which appeared in 1904. It was printed by W.B. Cooke of The Thoroton Press at Nottingham as, by that time, Robert White had disposed of that side of his business. Essentially a book for the browser, the seeker of the interesting snippet, the serious scholar may find it disappointing. It is bitty, much of it consists of extracts from longer documents and some of its contents are not dated. However, to carp at its omissions is less than generous. By its publication Robert White preserved much material that, at his death, would either have been dispersed or even lost.

The little that is known of Robert White's life outside his work and his writing can soon be told. After a time he re-married and set up home with his new wife and daughter at 1, Park Place. Unfortunately his second marriage was brief, his wife dying in 1871. Shortly afterwards his daughter married Mr. John Kirkland and moved to London. Robert White married again but once more was destined to be a widower as his third wife, Susan, pre-deceased him by five years. By then he had retired from business, disposing of his printing works and shop in 1898, when he was in his eightieth year. Although an octogenarian, Robert White's last years were not spent idly. As well as working on "Dukery Records" he still sold books. On his retirement, he transferred much of his stock from the shop to his home. At his death he had upwards of five thousand volumes on his shelves.

Great age brought inevitable weakness and following the death of his third wife on the 28th January, 1903 Robert White was looked after by his housekeeper, Mrs. Dwyer. After a few years of failing health he became seriously ill in the early weeks of 1908. His daughter returned home to care for him and was there at his death on the 1st. March. A friend, penning an obituary notice for a local newspaper,[9] summarised his achievements, "In his death Worksop has lost one of its most noteworthy tradesmen - one whose name will long be held in honour as its chief historian, and who made also for the town a notable name in the book and printing world which in years to come will grow in appreciation."

Notes and References

1. I was told this by Miss Winifred Boothroyd.
2. Kelly's Directory of Nottinghamshire, 1848.
3. See "A Long-forgotten Chapel," pages 34-42
4. The Retford and Gainsborough Times, 13 March, 1908.
5. Ibid.
6. James Hayward taught chemistry at the Pestalozzian School on Potter Street. He was an advocate of scientific methods of farming.
7. A copy of "The History of Roche Abbey"was priced at £100 at a book fair held in 2004.
8. Notes and Queries.
9. The Retford and Gainsborough Times, 6th March, 1908.

To be a Farmer's Boy.

During the first half of the 19th century, more Worksop men worked on local farms than followed any other occupation. In 1841 they numbered almost three hundred[1] and some had been so employed from their tenderest years. It was nothing for children as young as seven or eight to spend their days bird tenting. Samuel Stringfellow was only six when he began work for Mr. Hopkinson at Manton Farm while William Ward was but a year older when he started at Hawks' Nest Farm. For some this early beginning was the introduction to a life of toil on the land while others, after taking home their two shillings (l0p) a week for a year or two moved on to other employment.

At that time there were farms within the town itself, others were all around it, some of considerable extent. Exact numbers are difficult to determine. A directory of 1832[2] mentions just ten while in the edition of twelve years later, only seven are recorded. These figures are contradicted by the census returns of 1841 which include at least twenty eight people who are described as farmers. Later directory entries suggest that there were around thirty farms of various sizes within a three or four mile radius of Worksop. Among the largest, Castle Farm spread over six hundred and eighty acres and Rayton Farm five hundred and seventy. Others were almost as extensive while some of the men described as farmers in the census were little more than small holders, perhaps cultivating the odd acre and keeping a cow or two, a sty of pigs and a few chickens.

Despite the introduction of improved implements, especially during the second half of the century, farming remained hard work for both men and animals. Hours were long and for those who lived in the town and worked on one of the outlying farms these were supplemented by quite a long trudge to and from their places of labour. In this respect few, if any, equalled the record of Thomas Mason who, for sixty six years, lived in Worksop and worked at Osberton. Each week he walked about forty miles and it has been calculated that over his working life his mileage would have equalled one hundred and thirty seven thousand, two hundred and eighty, equivalent to five and a half times round the world.[3] As a young man he earned around 10s. (50p) a week and this would have risen to 15s. (75p), with a little more at harvest time, by the middle years of the century. Jack Ward worked for Mr. George Motley on Castle Farm and one day the master accosted the man, "Jack, I reckon thou's got wed?" "Yes, mester." "Well, two mouths tek more stopping than one and I shall raise thee wages two shillin' a week."[4] With such a wage, plus the extra few shillings that his wife and children could earn, it was adjudged that a family could subsist, "with strict economy" and "find clothing also, and pay rent."[5] The latter expense varied between £2 and £5 a year. It is not surprising that the question, "Could it (the family) lay anything by?" received the answer, "It is thought they could lay by nothing." They could, however, help supply the pot as most cottages had gardens, allotments were increasingly available as the century progressed and a pig would provide meat for a good part of the year. Never the less, good health, hard work and careful management were necessary for a family to just about keep its head above water. No wonder that the prospects of higher wages and shorter hours outweighed the possible dangers and lured a number of men from farm to colliery when coal began to be mined locally.

Farming around Worksop was mixed with more land being put to the plough than used for grazing. In 1834 about 6,500 acres were arable and 4,078 acres pasture[6] though the way in which a farmer worked his land depended on its location for there was a marked difference in the nature of the soil. Farms to the south and east of the town were on the sandy "forest" soil while those to the west were on the heavier clays. This basic difference was taken into consideration when arranging the categories in the annual ploughing match that was organised by the Labourers' Friend Society. There were separate events for the men who worked the clay land and those whose daily toil was on the lighter sandy soil.

For hundreds of years, until around the outbreak of World War 2 in 1939 horse power dominated local farms. Some of the larger ones needed between twenty and thirty horses to haul carts and wagons and pull ploughs and other implements. The scene on this picture is timeless: the patient team, the skilful ploughman and the pattern of immaculately turned furrows. (Picture by permission of Mr. R. Allsopp).

Wherever a man worked and whatever the soil, he would finish the day well weary as most of his tasks were manual. As the century progressed some machinery was introduced but muscular effort still predominated. With experience a man developed a pace and a rhythm that he could keep up all day and though to the casual observer he might appear to be almost idling, the amount that he achieved in that time was considerable. Most men used their own hand tools, a familiarity with grip, weight and balance tending towards greater comfort and efficiency. A long day's work left little time or energy for leisure activities. An hour in the garden, a half pint and a chat at the local would suffice most men though, from time to time, this simple routine was heightened by events of a more special nature.

One of these was the annual ploughing match organised by the Worksop Labourers' Friend Society. This took place in October of each year and was not only a day of contesting skill but also a pleasant social gathering. The society began in a small, localised way but gradually extended its area of activity. It was founded in 1840 by Mr. Henry Vessey Machin, Mr. James Hodgkinson and Mr. Henry Eddison, all of Gateford and it was at first called the Gateford Ploughing Society. After some twelve years of steadily growing support, the society changed its name to the one by which it was more generally known and increased the number of its competitions to include the whole range of farm work. Ploughing contests remained the core of the annual gathering but there were also prizes for shepherds raising the most lambs and for the man who had worked longest for one master.

There was a similar prize, too, for the single woman who had given the longest service as a farm servant with the same family. Competitions and prize givings over, the day ended in conviviality. In 1854 the dinner for the officers of the society and the farmers took place at the Red Lion Hotel where the diners were, "very liberally supplied with the various dainties in season and wines of the choicest vintage," while nearby, at the Bull Inn, "The labourers feasted to their hearts content."[7]

Though mere spectators at the ploughing matches, shepherds were able to show their skill at the regular sheep shearing competitions that were held locally. These were comparatively modest events, attracting a cluster of onlookers rather than the larger crowds of the ploughing matches. One such contest took place towards the end of May of 1888 under the arches of the Golden Ball Inn. The competitors had to shear five sheep within a three hour period, the quality of the work as well as the time being taken into consideration by the judges. On this occasion a man called Bland from Dinnington was the winner and so deft was he with the shears that it was the general opinion that he could have clipped at least two more sheep in the time allowed.[8]

Once its original, and more serious, business had been completed, the annual Statutes Fair was the one occasion when many farm workers had a few shillings in their pockets and the opportunity to spend them in pursuit of a good time. Traditionally, in Worksop, this was held on the second Wednesday of November, the day on which agreements between master and man expired and, consequently, on which work was sought for the next twelve months. Those looking for work stood on Bridge Street, near the market, usually wearing or holding some sign of any special skill that they might possess. A shepherd might carry his crook and a carter his whip. Prospective employers, both farmers and their wives, for house servants were hired in the same way, made their choice, wages and terms were discussed and if agreement was reached, the deed was confirmed with the payment of a "fastening penny" which by the middle of the 19th century, was usually a shilling (5p). Tradition has it that many of these coins finished the day in the tills of the public houses.

In 1854 business seems to have been brisk. "Our statutes for hired servants of both sexes took place on Wednesday, the 15th inst., and not withstanding the very rainy state of the weather during the preceding night, and on the morning, a great number of servants were in attendance, as well as masters and mistresses. We have been informed a tolerably large amount of hiring was effected, and at liberal wages."[9] Twenty or so years later the hiring activities of the day were in decline. In 1871 the local paper commented, "We believe very little was done in the shape of hiring so that we are unable to give any particulars as to wages."[10] Sixteen years later it reported similarly that, "actual business was small," though did give some details of wages that were agreed upon. On average boys received between £5 and £8 a year, men between £12 and £15 and best men £18 and £23. Girls were paid from £3-10s (£3.50) to £6 a year and women £8 to £13.[11]

Little by little, by the second half of the 19th century, the supremacy of the horse on local farms was being challenged by the steam powered traction engine. Although used for a variety of tasks, it was at its most impressive when providing power for a threshing drum, as seen in this picture. Few, if any, farmers could afford or had the need of a traction engine of their own and would hire one from a contractor. In this picture the threshing set belonged to the Worksop firm of Flamwell and Appley. Mr. T. Flamwell is standing on the left and the driver is Mr. Jack Green who later worked for the town council. (Picture by permission of Mrs. R.M. Stevens.)

Even though less hiring was done, the occasion continued to be popular as it was the one day of the year when the farm workers, especially the young ones, could forget their daily drudgery and look forward to enjoying themselves. "The trains brought in their usual quantum of lads and lasses, who appear to have come more for the holiday and to meet with old faces than for hiring purposes," so said the local paper.[12] Providing entertainment of various kinds, stalls and booths were set up in the market place and main streets. Reports speak of photographic galleries, shooting galleries, galvanic batteries, try your strength machines, boxing booths, gingerbread stalls and mock auctions. Doubtless there were other attractions too.

In 1871 a number of caravans holding Purchas's Wax Model Exhibition were in attendance. Although all of these enjoyed a certain amount of custom it was the tills of the public houses that rang most merrily. One observer described it as a, "thorough landlord's day," while another commented that, "Sir John Barleycorn had a few chivalrous sons, who paid homage at his shrine."[13] Crowded streets and jingling pockets naturally attracted a number of men described as, "the light fingered gentry," though their successes seemed few. One man, caught in the act, spent the next month in the house of correction. Some people tended to look down on the activities of the Statutes Fair but they didn't have to be up at dawn on every other day of the year with the prospect of many hours of hard, physical work, whatever the weather, before them. The farm worker certainly deserved his few hours of fun, even if he did regret it on the next day.

Worksop's cattle market was moved from Bridge Street to Memorial Avenue in 1900. Here, on Wednesday of each week local farmers bought and sold their livestock and passed the time of day with friends and neighbours. This photograph, taken around 1934, shows Mr. Luke Burton with his pedigree Friesian bull.

Their employers, the local farmers, were, on the whole, a shadowy group of men. Little, beyond their names, is known of many of them. As a class they weren't active in town affairs: they didn't feature regularly in the local press and, if any of them compiled a journal, it hasn't come to light. As with all farmers, prevailing economic conditions and the vicissitudes of the climate largely determined the prosperity of their endeavours. During the early years of the century, when the Napoleonic Wars were being fought, demand for food was high and prospects good. With the signing of peace in 1815, farming entered a period of depression which lasted for over twenty years, until around 1838, when conditions began to improve. This trend continued for the next forty years or so, a time when well-to-do farmers often enlarged their premises, sought to better their productivity by implementing the various scientific improvements that were being introduced and, generally, bore the look of well-satisfied prosperity. Such times rarely last and by 1878 signs of recession were becoming apparent. Thereafter a decline set in, prices fell and many farmers found it a continual struggle to make ends meet.[14]

In view of these uncertainties, it is perhaps surprising that some families stuck to the soil as long as they did, in some cases for generations. The best example of this is the Owtrams who farmed at Rayton for upwards of two hundred years. Last of the line was Henry Owtram who gave up the farm in 1885, just three years before his death. No other family could boast such longevity of tenure though some coped with the fluctuating fortunes of farming for a good number of years. Around 1851 Joseph Beard took over the water mill on the New Road (later Mansfield Road) and began to farm the adjacent acres. Fifty years later he was still in business, the mill cushioning, to some extent, the uncertain rewards of farming. A few more kept their hands to the plough for around thirty years. These included John Edeson of Sparken Hill and George Sudbury of Newgate Street. At the close of the century his farm was being managed by Mary Ann Sudbury, presumably his widow. Another was Thomas Arthur of the more distant Sloswick Farm. Several others, while not carrying on for so long, were certainly farming for over twenty years. Among them were John Kelk of Gateford Road, John Marsh of Lowtown, the Marshall family of Hawk's Nest, George Barlow of Sandy Lane and Matthew Beard of Holme Carr.[15]

Doubtless there were others, too. Some of these town addresses seem unlikely locations for farms nowadays but in the 19th century they were not unusual. One such urban farm was on Eastgate. The house stood on the south side of the street, near the Anchor Inn, the outbuildings and stackyard were almost opposite, close to St. John's Girls' School, while the land was a little distant, lying between the present day South Parade and Shepherds Avenue.[16] There may well have been other similar split-site farms in the town   It is fair to say that all these farmers and, indeed, many others who had worked the land for a number of years, would have experienced changes in method, in equipment and in preference of stock during their working lives.

The "golden age" of the middle years of the century was, in part, the outcome of the application of new thinking, of the greater use of scientific aids and the introduction of improved implements and machinery. That such developments were of interest to the farmers of Worksop and district is most likely as, in the fourth Duke of Portland, they

It looks as if half the town is there. Certainly women by the hundred, many with their children, flocked to the local pea fields for two or three weeks in July when the pea crop was ready for harvesting. The whole operation was organised by Mr. Kirk Dennis and it was said that peas harvested in Worksop on one day could be served in London hotels on the next.

had one of the leading advocates of improved farming as a near neighbour. He was described as, "The leader of this progress," who, "was always ready to make experiments in the interests of agriculture."[17] He was an early user of bones as a fertiliser and, "an energetic tile drainer." His greatest achievement, though a little distant from Worksop, was the transformation of the valley of the River Maun between Mansfield Woodhouse and Clipstone by means of the Flood Dykes. Where the Duke led, others followed. Colonel Mellish of Blyth introduced the growing of turnips to the district and after harvesting his own crop, gave samples of seeds to neighbouring farmers. At first, their efforts were not too successful, probably through ignorance in the correct ways of their cultivation. Once experience had remedied that drawback and once mechanical means of slicing them had been devised, turnips became a staple crop of local farms. They fed the livestock for a good four months of the year and made it possible to keep increased numbers. A farmer near Retford wrote that a farm of three hundred acres that at the beginning of the century could sustain fifty sheep; by the 1850's could feed up to seven hundred.[18] The turnip was the reason for this amazing increase. In fact, the prosperity enjoyed by Worksop's farmers during the years between 1838 and 1878 stemmed from the use of the draining tile, artificial fertilisers and the growth of the turnip.

One person credited with spreading these new ideas in farming practice was James Hayward. He was a chemist by training and taught at the Pestalozzian school on Potter Street. Sometime around 1850 he gave a series of lectures on scientific farming to an interested group meeting under the name of the Blyth Farmers' Club. In 1852 the substance of these talks was printed by Robert White, under the title, "Letters to Farmers." It was a book of some impact, the local paper commenting, "The result of this book was almost a revolution in local farming circles with regard to manuring and rotation of crops."[19] Perhaps there was a touch of exaggeration in these words though doubtless the book was read, its ideas mulled over and discussed wherever farmers gathered and some of its suggestions put into practice.

Throughout the 19th century, Worksop remained pre-eminently a market town. Although, by its end, more men worked below ground than in its fields, its weekly markets, both provision and cattle, still drew in the local farmers. Here they haggled over prices at the Corn Exchange, sold their stock in the cattle market and discussed the week's news as they sat over their mountainous dinners at the Lion or one of the other inns. For the greater part of the century the cattle market was held on the upper part of Bridge Street, running down to about as far as Castle Street. It was certainly no time for the Worksop matrons to do their shopping as beasts, sheep and horses virtually blocked the main street of the town. The situation improved in the 1870's when the market was transferred to a site between Newcastle Avenue and the river. There it remained until the end of the century when it was moved to the south side of the Canch and the imposing arcade buildings rose on the place that it had vacated.

This picture, taken in the opening years of the 20th century, illustrates a change that had already taken place in the work pattern of Worksop. For centuries the majority of local men had gained their livelihood from the land. By the time Ezra Taylor took this photograph of Manton Colliery, coal miners outnumbered farm workers in the town. (Picture by permission of Mr. R. Allsopp).

An ability to adapt to new developments and improved methods was necessary if a farmer was to prosper during good times and ride out the periods of recession. Change was the watchword. In the 1880's Henry Owtram would farm his land at

Rayton far differently from Francis Owtram in the 1830's. Apart from more extensive draining, the use of artificial fertilisers and the cultivation of turnips that have already been mentioned, the quality of the livestock at the latter date was much superior to that at the former. By then the Leicestershire sheep, or a cross between the Leicestershire and the Lincolnshire had completely replaced the native Forest breed. Shorthorns were the favoured breed of cattle while the pig had been transformed from, "a long-eared, coarse-offaled animal, difficult to fatten and unpalatable to eat," to an animal that was much more compact in appearance, "with small ears, short snout, deep in the sides and thigh, and short in the leg."[20] And, no doubt, it was more tasty, too.

Throughout the century the horse was vital to many farming activities. Some of the larger farms kept between twenty and thirty of them. Although an occasional ox was still at work in the early years [21] and steam engines were not unknown later on, the horse reigned supreme. Many were shires and some could still be seen at the plough or cart until the 1940's. By then, though, their day was really over; that of the tractor was in the ascendant.

Just as the successful farmer had to be progressive in his thinking, his workmen had to be adaptable in using new and improved implements. Nowhere was this more apparent than in harvesting. When Thomas Mason began his working days in 1800 the sickle was in general use. Gradually it was superseded by the scythe though, for a time, both were in use simultaneously. A newspaper report of 1854 speaks of the, "scythe and the sickle of the reapers," being, "still in active operation,"[22] Ten years later the scythe dominated the harvest fields though signs of the future were already apparent as, by 1867, the Duke of Portland had four mowing machines at work. Twenty years on from then, machinery was a common sight. The local paper commented, "The harvest work as performed nowadays differs very much from what was current a dozen or 20 years ago. Improved reapers have come into use, each season seeing a fresh improvement in the tackle."[23] Perhaps the major improvement was the introduction of the combined reaper and binder, the first of which was seen in the late 1870's on Mr. Sydney Smith's farm at Burnt Leys. Its performance aroused great interest in the farming fraternity and market day chat often centred on the speed with which the harvest could be gathered using the new machines. It was regarded by some as a local record when two reapers and a reaper and binder at Osberton cut two hundred acres of corn in six days. Others claimed even greater achievements.

One consequence of this growing use of machinery was the lessening need for casual labour at harvest time. Among the first to be affected were the gangs of itinerant Irish men who, for years, had sought work on local farms. "They literally come in shoals in quest of employment," noted a local paper in 1848.[24] Following the coming of the reaper, there would be less chance of them finding work. Not that all prospects of earning a few extra shillings disappeared. Help was always needed at potato picking time. "The digging and collecting of potatoes in this district is just now finding employment for a large number of hands - some men and the rest women and children." So it was reported in 1887.[25] This was followed by the optimistic note, "The crops are good and heavy, and potatoes will probably be cheap this winter."

Towards the end of the century an even greater number of townspeople, again mainly women and children, flocked to the fields in high summer to gather in the pea harvest. For about a fortnight in July they were at work by first light and continued until around noon when the day's crop had been gathered. Its disposal was highly organised and the man responsible for this for a number of years was Mr. Kirk Dennis. A farmer himself, he also bought up the crops of other local farmers and arranged for their transportation to London and other regional markets. After a fortnight's picking in 1901, one hundred and fifty truck loads - each holding three tons - had already been despatched from Worksop station. So speedy was the system that peas picked at Worksop in the morning could be on sale that same evening in London and served for lunch on the following day. The average daily earnings of the pea pickers varied between 4s. (20p) and 5s. (25p) which, over a week, would be as much, if not more, than the wage of the man of the house. A good harvest, too, meant a welcome boost to the income of the farmers, many of them struggling to make a living in the time of agricultural depression of the 1880's and '90's. Not for nothing was Mr.Dennis known as the "Pea King."[26]

Casual work apart, when the fields were thronged with pea and potato pickers, the call "to be a farmer's boy" grew less strong as the century progressed. Alternate forms of work, often with higher wages and more free time proved more attractive than the day in, day out drudgery on the farm. This was especially so in Worksop where the nearby collieries were usually in need of labour. When, in 1907 Manton colliery became fully operational, more men than ever were drawn from the field to the coal face. In Worksop "collier" had long replaced "agricultural labourer" as the most frequently recorded occupation of the town's menfolk. By 1891 the number of the latter was about a hundred less than it had been fifty years earlier. Never the less, as the twentieth century dawned, those who remained on the land could expect to earn between 15s. (75p) and £1 a week plus a little more at harvest and other busy times. With care and reasonable management this was just about liveable on but allowed for few extras.

In this respect the man was little worse off than his master. Times remained hard though perhaps not as bad as one Nottinghamshire farmer had forecast, "I made money, now I'm losing it, and I'm going out before I lose more. There is no prospect."[27] However, for those who were satisfied to just about break even, there was still a livelihood in farming and there were still those who strove to achieve it. Although work and worry were the everyday companions of Worksop's farmers, there were occasions when they could set them aside for a few hours. These were the days of the local agricultural shows. The best known were held at Clumber and Welbeck though the one gaining the widest support was held at Whitsuntide of 1910 in the town itself. This was the annual show of the Nottinghamshire Agricultural Society. These events were for the farmers what the ploughing matches and sheep shearings were for the farm workers. They were occasions where prime livestock could be shown, new equipment and machinery examined, friends met and the conviviality of the refreshment tent enjoyed. Though worries could not be completely forgotten, they could at least be shared and future prospects discussed though even the most far sighted would be hard put to foresee some of the further changes in farming that the new century was to bring.

Notes and References

1. 1841 Census Returns.

2. W.White. Directory of Nottinghamshire. 1832.

3. The Newark Advertiser, 17th October 1866.

4. M.J.Jackson. Victorian Worksop. 1992

5. Poor Law Commission Enquiry. 1834.

6. Ibid.

7. The Nottingham Review, 27th October, 1854.

8. The Retford & Gainsborough Times, 1st, June, 1888.

9. The Nottingham Review, 17th November, 1854.

10. The Retford & Gainsborough Times, 11th November, 1871.

11. Ibid.

12. Ibid.

13. The Nottingham Review, 17th November, 1854.

14. The chapter on agriculture in the Victoria County History of Nottinghamshire, vol.2 by W.H.R.Curtler.

15. Various 19th century directories.

16. Letter in the Worksop Guardian, 23rd February, 1968.

17. W.H.R.Curtler. The Victoria County History of Nottinghamshire Vol. 2.

18. Aspects of Nottinghamshire Agricultural History. Various Contributors 1989.

19. The Worksop Guardian, 6th March, 1908.

20. W.H.R.Curtler. The Victoria County History of Nottinghamshire Vol. 2.

21. Emma Wilmot, a talented artist, who lived in Sparken House in the 1840's made a number of sketches of farming scenes. One of these showed an ox harnessed to a plough.

22. The Nottingham Review, 1st September, 1854.

23. The Retford & Gainsborough Times, 19th August, 1887.

24. The Nottingham Review, 4th August, 1848.

25. The Retford & Gainsborough Times, 4th November, 1887.

26. The Worksop Guardian, 19th July, 1901.

27. W.H.R.Curtler. The Victoria County History of Nottinghamshire Vol. 2.

PICTURE SUPPLEMENT, 4
FIRST BUS IN WORKSOP.

Although the small group of sightseers on this picture are probably seeing a motor bus for the first time in their lives, their attention seems to have been drawn from it to Amos Emblin and his camera as he took this photograph. The year was 1906 and the bus, which belonged to the Ryknield Motor Co. Ltd. of Burton on Trent was on a promotional tour, hoping to attract a buyer from a local authority or a business man with an eye to the future. It did neither at Worksop. The fact that its bonnet is open suggests that it might have broken down, which would not have recommended it to any local buyer.

Several years elapsed before any similar vehicle again ran along the main streets. In the meantime, an occasional horse drawn bus plodded its way through the town, while transport to nearby villages was provided by the carrier's cart.

A Worksop Diary.

A diary from the past can be a most fascinating and fruitful source of information for the local historian. It can also be most frustrating. Such is one of 1876, produced by Letts, Son and Co. Limited and partly completed by a Worksop man. Until the end of July he made daily entries but also plastered the book with cuttings from the local and national press, articles from a variety of magazines and items of printed ephemera. The entries are invariably short, often terse and sometimes meaningless to a present day reader: clearly a personal record rather than an account of events and opinions set down for the benefit of posterity.

Had Joseph Garside stood on the earlier canal bridge and looked down Priorswell Road, with the exception of the Priory Church, he would have been the owner of all that he saw. The gateway on the right led to his brewery, the road to the left, Garside Street, to his timber yard while the roadside cottages housed his work people. The Hollingworth family lived in one of these cottages and it is highly likely that is where George Hollingworth wrote his diary.

So little did the compiler expect anyone else to see his journal that he did not even write his name on it or, indeed, include any helpful clues to its authorship in its contents. Fortunately, it has been rescued from anonymity by a later owner who wrote on the front cover, in ball point pen, "Compiled by Mr. Hollingsworth Gateford Rd Worksop." Reference to directories and the census returns has revealed that he could have been Mr. George Henry Hollingworth who, in 1891, lived at 144, Gateford Road. Supporting this identification, though not too positively, is a poem of Christmas greetings written in pencil on a loose sheet in the diary. It is headed, "To George Moffitt 1876," and signed, "Your loving Cousin George."

According to the 1891 census, George Hollingworth was forty eight, married to Elizabeth who was fifteen years his junior and they had a one year old son, also called George. He was born at Eckington, in Derbyshire and earned his livelihood as a wood turner, more specifically a spade shaft finisher. In this he followed his father who, when the family moved to Worksop around 1850, was said to have introduced that particular line of the timber trade to the town. He worked for Mr. Joseph Garside, whose extensive wood yard spread over much of the ground between the canal to the north and the Priory Church to the south. It was bounded on the west by Priorswell Road and here the family lived in a terrace house in what was locally known as Garside's Yard. At the time of the 1871 census, George was still at home, living with his mother and father, his elder sister Kezia and his younger brother Joseph, who was also a spade shaft maker. It is likely that it was in this house that he compiled his diary.

All looks very peaceful on this photograph of 1906. It was far different thirty years earlier, in 1876, when an angry crowd gathered outside the Lion Hotel on the occasion of a parliamentary bye-election. Anger turned to violence and considerable damage was done to nearby property and a number of people were injured. Peace was not restored until troops were sent from Sheffield. Hollingworth's sympathies, as he recorded the events of the day, were with the offenders rather than the forces of law and order.

Firstly, it must be said, that for the latter day reader, it is a most disappointing book. In the main it consists of a list of events though it is not clear whether the writer attended them all. Personal thoughts and opinions rarely intrude and autobiographical details are sparse. He never mentions his work, what it was and, indeed, whether he ever did any. However, three things are apparent. He was a staunch liberal in politics, a Methodist in faith and a loyal member of the Independent Order of the Good Templars. These interests dominated both his leisure time and the entries that he made in his diary. Of the first, an event of some notoriety happened in Worksop in 1876 and George Hollingworth's comments on it are perhaps the most fascinating of all he wrote. The occasion was a riot that broke out on the day of a Parliamentary bye-election, the 24th February. Most surviving accounts, certainly those in the local press, favoured the conservative cause and the forces of law and order. George Hollingworth's sympathies, on the contrary, were firmly with the other side; the oppressed as he saw them.

Briefly what happened was this. On the 11th February Hollingworth recorded the funeral of Lord Galway. "Minute bell tolled at noon – Lord Galway buried at Harworth – 2 miles from Serlby Hall. Great crowds attended the funeral: Lady Galway followed". He had been the member of Parliament for Bassetlaw and it was his death that caused the bye-election. Both the major parties nominated candidates and they were joined by the Worksop barber and local character Job Ebenezer Cartledge, a self styled representative of the working man. Twenty nine years had passed since there had last been a contested election in Bassetlaw. Thus many, including the recently enfranchised working men, were voting for the first time. As well as that, there was a popular local tradition that on election day the laws of the land did not apply: it was a time of liberty and license. That the preliminary skirmishing was lively was obvious from Hollingworth's comments, partisan as they were. Mr. Fox Bristow, the Liberal candidate, was, "At Worksop (and spoke) from the Bull Hotel window (at) 5.30. immense cheering," while the conservative candidate fared quite differently. "Mr. Denison at (Corn) Exchange - Garside introduced him - Tylden Wright chair - Wouldn't hear him. Booing shouting disorderly meeting and ended in discomfiture for the Blues." Excitement continued to run high until polling day when the situation erupted out of control and enthusiasm degenerated to violence and vandalism. Hollingworth summarised these depredations, "The Lion Hotel - windows were smashed, much noise. After dark a party of big boys played sad havoc with windows in Bridge, Park & Potter Sts. 2 companies of 19th Rgt came from Shefd."

Apparently the day had begun comparatively quietly though not without its intimations of impending trouble and by four o'clock a crowd of upwards of one thousand had gathered outside the Lion Hotel, the Conservatives' headquarters. At first they were content to shout and hoot but soon were stirred to more belligerent action. What caused this change is not clear. Some said that various objects were thrown from the Lion onto the crowd but this was never proved. Whatever the provocation, about a hundred men rushed into the yard of the hotel, attacking several men who were standing there and tried to gain access. In this they were frustrated and, after a while, began to wreak their vengeance against the building rather than its occupants. Soon its windows were shattered while the police, who had been reinforced for the day, were so heavily outnumbered that they were powerless to prevent the damage. Though they tried to control the crowd and protect individual victims of its wrath their efforts were largely unsuccessful and several officers, including Superintendent Blaisdale, were injured before they eventually withdrew to the comparative safety of the police station. Following their departure, the "big lads" mentioned by Hollingworth extended the area of their spoliations. Gangs of youths and young men ranged between the Catholic church on Park Street and the Town Dyke Bridge that crossed the River Ryton on Bridge Street, smashing shop and house windows of known Conservative sympathisers and attacking public houses, irrespective of the political alliance of the landlords. These activities, described by the judge at the subsequent trial as, "a reign of terror," continued unchecked until the arrival of the ten o'clock train from Sheffield, Alighting from it, a detachment of the 19th Foot, the Princess of Wales Own, sixty eight men in all, formed up on the platform and, with fixed bayonets, marched into town. This show of force dampened the bravado of the rioters and they soon drifted away to their homes. By midnight the town was quiet as the soldiers mounted guard on the Lion Hotel.

Next morning, Hollingworth walked into town to see the damage, "at 8,30 we went up and saw the havoc.. .. .. Glaziers at work. Soldiers keeping guard at Lion - Corn Exchange turned into barrack room. Soldiers to stay until Monday, Rioters before the magistrates. Papers full of Riots at Worksop." He also, no doubt sadly, recorded the result of the election. The Liberal candidate lost by a mere one hundred and eighty seven votes. Memories of the election rankled with George Hollingworth for many days. While neither approving nor condemning the violence and destruction that took place he deplored the use of soldiers in stopping it. Like others in the town, he felt that the disturbances had just about run their course and that the arrival of the troops prolonged them. He scornfully referred to Mr.Charles Tylden-Wright, the magistrate who summoned the military help as "Tiddlem Wrong," "Tiddlem Wrong," he wrote, "he made a song, and sent to Sheffield for the Soldiers." The presence of the red coats and the sight of the fixed bayonets clearly irked and it must have been with some satisfaction that on Sunday, the 27th February he completed his entry for the day with, "Soldiers went back to Shefd. heartily sick of Worksop."

Fourteen men faced the magistrates on the day after the riot. Of these, one was discharged though by the time the court re-convened in the following week, another fifteen had been arrested. The number was reduced to twenty three when the Assizes sat on the 24th March. All were young; most were in their twenties though four were still in their teens and three in their thirties. All were working men, fifteen of them colliers. George Hollingworth clearly felt that the arrests had been indiscriminate, "Bobbies throng running the rioters in. Anybody would do," he wrote. Of the first day of the trial at the magistrates' court, his sole comment was, "Slaughter of the Innocents." Of the second, he was slightly more informative, "Col. Holden (the chief constable) here. 21 prisoners taken off in two bus loads by 7 (o'clock) train." On the 3rd. March he mentioned efforts to raise money for their defence. "George Warburton collecting on behalf of the "rioters" Q.C. Fund met with much success," and on the following day, "Collections are being made at Shireoaks Colliery £40. Garsides, Cuttons, Caudwells, Canal Road." These three firms were timber merchants. As a result of these collections, all the prisoners were represented at the Assizes, though to little effect. All were found guilty, some having to serve six months in prison with hard labour, others four months and the rest two. Hollingworth somewhat prosaically recorded. "Nottingham Assizes. Baron Huddlestone Judge Worksop Electionists tried. Judgement deferred (sic) till Sat. at 10 am." Of that judgement he made no mention though it must have both distressed and angered him. He spent the greater part of the day on which it was made in Sheffield, calling on friends and rounding off the evening with a visit to the Music Hall to see Mr. C.H. Duval's "Odds and Ends," which he somewhat curtly summarised as, "Clever Ent" (entertainment). As a post script to the bye-election and its sad consequences, the local Liberals held a grand dinner on the 18th April in Retford Town Hall. The recently defeated candidate, Mr Henry Fox Bristowe, Q.C., was the guest of honour and with him on the top table were the Rt. Hon. Robert Lowe, the Duke of St. Albans and a number of party supporters who were prominent in the district. Despite the disappointment of the election result, Hollingworth noted that, "The speeches were very happy and well received."

George Hollingworth was a staunch Methodist and entries in the diary suggest that he attended the United Free Methodist chapel on Potter Street. When the family came to Worksop around 1850 this chapel of 1837 was in use. After it had been replaced in 1875 Hollingworth recorded in his diary that photographs of the earlier building could be bought for 6d. (2.5p) each This illustration is probably one of those souvenir pictures.

Like many others of his time, George Hollingworth shared his zeal for the liberal party with his dedication to his chapel for he was a staunch Methodist. Which particular denomination of Methodism he belonged to he does not make clear for he mentions the activities of all three that were then established in Worksop. These were the Wesleyans, the Primitive Methodists and the United Methodists. The diary does, however, give the impression that it was the latter that he favoured. If so, he would have taken his place for Sunday worship in a brand new chapel. Following their secession from the Wesleyans, the group later known as the United Methodists began meeting in the town in the early 1830's. By 1837 they had built a chapel in Potter Street but it was small in size and modest in appearance and soon inadequate for their needs. It was its replacement, on the same site and opened in 1875, that Hollingworth wrote of in his diary and where on the 4th February, "Rev John Gutteridge of Manchester gave one of his grand lectures "The Bible tested and triumphant" Councillor Woodcock, Shef(field) in the chair with Messrs Alf(red) Gutteridge and Hartley. Rev. J.E. Moore (Congregational minister) & Mr. T. Parkinson (Primitive Methodist local preacher) spoke - large audience," Should any of those present have nostalgic feelings for their former chapel, an entry a few days later noted that photographs of it were available at 6d. (2.5p) each.

George Hollingworth was an active member of the Good Templars friendly society. It was one of a number of organisations in Victorian times that advocated self help and temperance. The tea meeting was one of the ways that encouraged the latter. This hand bill advertised one of these occasions: tea and an evening of entertainment and all for one shilling (5p.).

The new and larger United Free Methodist chapel of 1875 was the first of three non-conformist places of worship built in the town within a four year period. In the following year the Independents (Congregationalists) moved to a new chapel on Bridge Place. This was somewhat tersely noted by Hollingworth on the 18th July, "Opening new Independent Chapel Bridge St. Rev Rogers London, preached at 3 and 7. Tea at 5. Miss Redfern at the organ." He obviously thought that the event merited a more detailed description as he cut out a report from a local paper and pasted it into his diary. The trio was completed in 1879 when the Primitive Methodists opened their new chapel on John Street. Sadly, not one of these buildings now stands.

Even if George Hollingworth's loyalties were primarily to the United Free Methodists, he didn't ignore the activities of the other chapels. A celebrated preacher, an anniversary, a special tea or such event would attract him, irrespective of denomination. As early in the year as the 9th February he attended a "Coffee Supper" at the Primitive Methodist chapel on Newgate Street. Seven tray holders attended to the needs of the "52 (who) sat down and it was very enjoyable. 15/10d. (79p) profit." Spiritual nourishment was also provided as the "Rev. George Watson, Circuit Minister, preached an admirable sermon - in his own pec(u)l(ia)r way." Later in the month, on the 29th, he attended the, "Tea

& 'Elijah' Service of Song by T.K. Longbottom," at the Wesleyan chapel. This occupies the same site as the present chapel; it was built in 1863 and destroyed by fire in 1969. "Well sung and interesting," was his comment on the performance. Just after Easter, on the 20th April, Hollingworth's dedication to Methodism took him to Eckington, his birthplace and boyhood home. Here he was present at the opening services of the Wesley Memorial Chapel: splendid occasions at which he heard Dr. Gervase Smith, the President of the Wesleyan Conference, preach in the afternoon and Dr. Morley Punshon, a former president, in the evening and, no doubt, enjoying the tea that was served in between at 5 o'clock. Never one to waste words, his summary of so memorable a day was, "Good choir 8 anthems. Beautiful building."

Like Worksop, Eckington experienced a spate of chapel building in the 1870's. A year before the Wesleyan chapel was opened, in 1875 the United Free Methodists completed one of their own. It was a large, imposing building and presumably the one that Hollingworth referred to, "Saw the Top Chapel. newly opened, new organ £230."

Last in the sequence, the Primitive Methodists moved to new premises in 1877 and, of the three chapels, theirs is the only one still in use. George Hollingworth spent three days at Eckington on this occasion. He called on relations and friends was up early each morning and walked miles to look at collieries, foundries, brickworks, quarries, kilns and a pug mill on a tour that would have delighted present day industrial archaeologists. His wanderings finally ended at Creswell station where he caught the 5.30 train back to Worksop, travelling along the recently opened Midland Railway line from Mansfield.

The entries in the diary for most Sundays contain details of services at local chapels and the inference is that Hollingworth attended them. There is little evidence, though, that he often took part in the various week night activities that were then such a regular part of chapel life. His evenings were largely taken up in temperance work. Unfortunately his cryptic references do not make the extent of his involvement too clear. That he was a member of the Hope of Worksop Lodge, No. 2604, of the Independent Order of Good Templars is obvious but there are also suggestions that he was a Rechabite as well. The Independent Order of Rechabites was founded in 1835 as a friendly society for working men who were pledged abstainers from alcoholic drinks. They took their unusual name from an Old Testament tribe who abjured wine, neither planted nor possessed vineyards and who lived in tents.[1] Their Victorian namesakes referred to their branches as tents and it is the use of this word in his diary that implies that Hollingworth was a member. On four occasions he mentions a "tent night." These occurred at fortnightly intervals, on Saturdays, and were meetings when regular subscriptions were paid into the sickness and funeral funds and disbursements paid out to those entitled to receive them. On the tent night on the 12th February he noted that there were, "2 persons sick." "Quarter nights" supplemented the routine "tent nights" and on the one held on the 1st. July, "3 propositions," presumably of new members, were received. There was just a hint in Hollingworth's entry of three days earlier that he might have been an officer of the society, he was certainly a helper. "Wednesday, 28th June, Obt(ain)d 3 propositions for Rechabite tent, and delivered the summonses for Quarter night July 1st."

If Hollingworth's connections with the Rechabites were somewhat tenuous, there was no doubt of his involvement with the Good Templars for references in his diary are frequent even if details are sparse. The Independent Order of Good Templars was founded in the United States of America and introduced into England in 1868. Its spread was rapid though its popularity was not general. By 1873 a lodge had been formed in Worksop. This bore the number 2,604 and the name "Hope of Worksop." By 1876 it had already held one hundred and forty meetings, boasted one hundred and twenty four enrolled members though only had just over £3 in its treasury. It was of this lodge that George Hollingworth was a member. He first mentioned its activities on the 1st, February when he wrote, "'Hope of Worksop, Social Tea - games & c. good attendance." The local paper was slightly more informative in its report though it gave no indication what the single letter c stood for. It described the refreshments as a tea supper, stated that the event took place in, "their lodge room in Potter Street," and that members from a second Worksop lodge, the Spread Oak, were present. The evening was spent in a "social manner" and as this included a short address by Bro. H. Millard from Retford, the inference is that it was of a predominantly serious nature.[2] Thus, at the June meeting, a member read an extract from a sermon while Sister Peck, "recited in excellent manner 'A Scene at the Door'." As well as entertainment and the refreshments, business invariably occupied time at these meetings. Arrangements were made for future activities, reports read, new members might be initiated and applicants prepared for such an occasion.

A great day for the Hope of Worksop Lodge was Whit. Monday of 1876 when it hosted the quarterly meeting of the Nottinghamshire District Lodge. George Hollingworth wasted few words in recording the event in his diary. "Good Templars District Meeting to be held at Worksop. Jas. B. George in full swing, 150 to tea. Capital meeting at 7." Though such brevity was not unusual with him, on this occasion it was probably more justified as he did not attend it. He was at Sheffield with a group of friends, mingling with the holiday crowds and listening to the bands in Norfolk Park and the Botanical Gardens. A newspaper report which he cut out and mounted in his diary gives a more detailed account of the proceedings at Worksop. They began at 11.am when local lodge members walked in procession to the station, led by a drum and fife band and with a large banner depicting the Good Samaritan at their head. Their number augmented by delegates arriving on the 12.35 train, the procession re-formed and marched through the town to the Corn Exchange. While refreshments were being enjoyed within, the banner was hung in the entrance to the building where it was, "the admiration of all who saw it." A business meeting occupied the afternoon though all who wanted, and paid the necessary 9d. (4p) could sample the tea. The evening meeting ran from seven o'clock until ten and consisted of "several earnest addresses" interspersed by "several of Sankey's melodies," Mr. W, Ellis "presiding at the harmonium."

The success of the meeting led to an increase in membership of the two Worksop lodges and raised both spirits and aspirations. This was followed by a decision that the lodges should jointly apply for a charter to acquire their own premises, a Temple, as a centre for their activities. Hollingworth does mention this application on the 20th June but ceased making regular entries soon afterwards and so its outcome is not known.

With his concern for politics together with his involvement with his chapel and the Good Templars, it would be reasonable to think that George Hollingworth's leisure time was well filled. Occasional entries in his diary, however, suggest that his interests were even wider. There is little doubt that he had an appreciative ear for music. He pasted a number of concert programmes into his diary and, from time to time, was one of the audience. On the 25th March he travelled to Sheffield on the 12 noon train and, after making several calls, went to the, "Albert Hall Orchestral Concert, 35 performers." This began at 3 pm and, later in the day, he sampled somewhat lighter fare when he went to a music hall. Thus, both uplifted and amused, he returned to Worksop on the 11 o'clock train. If music was an occasional delight, then reading was an everyday pleasure. His diary is striking evidence of this for there isn't a single page that hasn't a cutting from a newspaper or a magazine stuck onto it. In fact the printed extracts often exceed and occasionally obscure the written entries and, it must be admitted, they are sometimes more interesting. Not that Hollingworth confined his reading to such ephemeral publications, he clearly had time for more weighty matters. On the 15th February he enjoyed a lecture given at the Mechanics' Institute by the Revd. Arthur Minsell on "Charles Dickens, a tribute."

Though there is no reference to taking part in any sport or, indeed, of watching any, he was interested enough to record the result of the boat race when, on the 8th April, he wrote, "Cambridge won," Later, on the 27th June, he noted that the Varsity cricket match was in progress at Lords, Cricket was his main sporting interest as there are several comments on the fortunes of the Nottinghamshire county team and one or two on Yorkshire's. Usually these are just a matter of jotting down scores or results though on one occasion he goes beyond the mere statistical when, on the 18th July, he wrote that Dick Daft's benefit match was being played at Trent Bridge. On the following day he added that teams representing the north and south of the country were taking part. Though Derbyshire born, Hollingworth's loyalties were primarily with Nottinghamshire. He not only mentioned them more than other counties but also stuck a photograph of the team into his diary.

As for the rest, there is little to say. On Monday, the 31st. July, having noted that, "17-3d.(86p) collected from 'Young Oak' to go to Grimsby & Cleethorpes with adults," he laid down his pen, never to add another word, or, at least, one that could be read as the remaining pages are completely pasted over with cuttings and similar ephemera.

Hardly anything can be written with any certainty of the later activities of George Hollingworth. He is not mentioned in the 1881 census returns so, presumably, he had left the town. Ten years later he was back, living at 144, Gateford Road. By then he was married though perhaps only recently as he had a one year old son. His wife was born at West Ham and the thought arises that Hollingworth might have been living and working in that part of the country while away from Worksop, That can be no more than supposition. What is certain is that by 1890 he was back, employed at his old trade of wood turner and spade shaft finisher. His days at the lathe were, however, limited.

The Worksop Mechanics Institute, originally founded in 1832 and revived in 1852, was chiefly known in the town for its library and reading room. These were based in two rooms at the back of the Town Hall. Although there is only a passing reference to the Institute in his diary, it is an organisation with which Hollingworth must have been in sympathy and he may well have been a member. By 1892 such speculation can end for in that year he was appointed its librarian. For a man of his inclinations, the work among the books and periodicals must have been an occupation that he relished but unfortunately it was only of short duration.

On the 16th December, 1895 the Worksop Urban District Council constituted itself a library authority, taking over the stock of the Mechanics' Institute. It decided to advertise the post of librarian and from the twenty two applicants Mr. Henry Wortley Latham, a former grocer, was appointed. It is not known if Hollingworth applied for the job. An occasional mention in local directories suggests that he spent his later years as a coal dealer. Hopefully further research will reveal more about this interesting person who, like so many others, started a diary but did not complete it and, in what he wrote, posed many more questions than he satisfactorily answered.

Notes and References

1. Jeremiah, Chapter 35, Verses 1-11.

2. The Retford and Gainsborough Times, 5 February, 1876.

PICTURE SUPPLEMENT, 5
BRIDGE PLACE.

Ezra Taylor was Worksop's best known photographer in the opening years of the 20th century. As a young man, he was in business as early as 1890 when, in an advertisement, he invited "attention to his Specimens of First Class Photography in all its various branches." At first his studio was located in the Cattle Market but he soon moved to more suitable premises on Bridge Place.

For twenty years or so, few outdoor events in the town were unrecorded by his camera; views of most streets were similarly captured. A number of his pictures have been used to illustrate this book and the one above is typical of them. Interestingly composed and clearly photographed, it shows Bridge Place looking northwards towards Victoria Square. On the left is the Dallas Yorke block, so called to commemorate the maiden name of the Duchess of Portland. Beyond it, over the canal bridge, are the offices of the Worksop and Retford Brewery Company. Across the road is the Watson Road corner and then the Prince of Wales buildings, fondly known in the town as "Kipper Row."

The Blind Squire.

If anyone had a bad word to say about George Savile Foljambe of Osberton Hall, it has not been handed down to posterity. Without exception the testimonies of his contemporaries have been favourable. "A friend of the poor, a good landlord, and a kind and benevolent country gentleman," is but one of many that have survived.[1]

Like many country houses, Osberton Hall has undergone a number of changes in appearance. It was built by George Savile Foljambe's grandfather, enlarged by his father and further extended by his son. This picture showed how it looked after the second modification and, indeed, still does today.

He was born on the 4th June, 1800, the son of John Savile Foljambe, whose father, Francis Ferrand Foljambe, had added the Osberton estates to his already extensive property in Derbyshire and Yorkshire. When George was five his father died and the young boy became heir to his grandfather. At this time workmen were busy at Osberton, virtually rebuilding and adding a massive four columned portico to the rather modest house that was built for Francis Foljambe when he inherited the property in the 1770's.[2] However, it was not its appearance that was the most interesting feature of the house, it was some of its contents for Francis Foljambe had assembled one of the finest collections of British birds in the land. Though less appealing to a young boy, a number of antiquities were also displayed in the house, pride of place being an altar piece that was thought to have come from Beauchief Abbey and which depicted the matyrdom of Thomas a Becket.

Indications are that George's main interest was focused on the stables rather than the museum for he became a fine horseman and developed a life long passion for the hunt. Sadness, however, was never long absent in his life and intruded again in

1814 when his grandfather, Francis Ferrand Foljambe, died. Thus, at fourteen, George became the squire of Osberton and the master of the various Foljambe properties. Doubtless there were those about him to advise and help in the consequent matters of estate management. Such responsibilities did not occupy all his time as he still found opportunities for the chase and so skilful did he become in his favoured sport that in 1822 he assumed the mastership of the local hunt, a position he held for over twenty years. Though generally known as the Grove, it is not known when it was first given that name but it was most likely during Mr. Foljambe's mastership as his kennels were at that village.

However much he was inclined to horse, hound and hunt, he still found time to discharge what he regarded as his public duties. In 1826, at what seems a very young age for such a position, he served as High Sheriff of the county while eleven years later he contested the North Nottinghamshire seat in a parliamentary election. Holding what have been described as, "good old Whig principles,"[3] he stood as the Liberal candidate though was not successful.

Scofton church was built in 1833 both as an act of commemoration by G.S. Foljambe for his wife who had died at the close of 1831 and as a place of worship for the families who lived on the estate. When complete, it was dedicated by the Archbishop of York. Twenty five years later, the remains of Mrs. Foljambe which had been interred in the church at Sturton-le-Steeple were brought to Scofton and placed in a specially constructed vault.

By then, in 1837, George Foljambe was already a widower. His marriage was short, lasting a mere two years, and in that time he experienced joy in the birth of a son and sadness in the death of his wife. She was Harriett Milner, daughter of Sir William Milner and the couple were married in 1828. On the 9th April, 1830 their son, Francis John

Savile Foljambe, was born and by the end of that year Harriett was dead. Her funeral took place on the 4th January, 1831 at Sturton-le-Steeple, the nearest village on the Foljambe estates with its own church. This lengthy journey of the cortege, combined with his natural grief, may well have sparked an idea in Mr. Foljambe's mind that led to a project that was to occupy much of his time during the next two years. He decided to build a church as an act of commemoration for his dead wife and as a more convenient place of worship for his estate workers and their families. A site was chosen across the River Ryton in the tiny village of Scofton, and Ambrose Poynter was appointed architect. Described as, "a remarkable building,"[4] it was built in the Norman style, simply and without excessive ornamentation. Progress was speedy and by 1833 the church was ready for dedication by the Archbishop of York. Twenty five years elapsed before Mrs. Foljambe's remains were brought from Sturton and re-interred in a vault in the newly built church.

Though an Anglican himself, Mr Foljambe was not averse to giving a little assistance to the non-conformists. Around the time that the walls of Scofton church were rising a small group of poor, working men in nearby Worksop were striving to build a place of worship. They were members of a recently established Primitive Methodist society. Having to watch every penny, their Newgate Street chapel was small, basic and functional, mainly built by the members from materials that were either second hand or begged. Responding to their appeal, Mr. Foljambe provided them with timber for the roof.[5] That he was generous by nature is obvious from numerous examples. When the railway was being built through his land, he was so impressed by the behaviour of the navvies that he ordered his gamekeepers to shoot sufficient hares to give one to each of the sixty or more men engaged on the work.[6] In the same year, on his 48th birthday, he provided an, "ample dinner of good old English fare of roast beef and plum pudding,"[7] for the inmates of the workhouse and those receiving outdoor relief. About two hundred and fifty people enjoyed the meal and, as an account of the occasion stated, "It is impossible for words adequately to make known the gratification felt by each individual who was the recipient of the bounty of this kind English gentleman." The same report ends with the poignant words, "We sincerely wish that Mr. Foljambe could have been blessed with his eyesight, to have witnessed for himself, the smiling faces…"[8]

He had lost his vision in 1845 and endured blindness for the remaining third of his life. This forced him to give up the mastership of the Grove Hunt and on the 2nd. of March of that year, the hounds upon which he had lavished such care hunted together for the last time. That was a sad day though a worse one was to come. On the 4th April the hounds were sold by auction at the kennels at Grove. So high was their reputation and so superlative their quality that they raised 3,574 guineas, a considerable price for the time. Chief among the purchasers were Lord Galway and Lord Henry Bentinck. A month later, on the 8th May, his horses were sold at Tattersall's at Newmarket. They realised £3,012 - 4 - 0d. (£3,012.20). Sad as his blindness and its consequences must have made him, he was far from bowed down by his handicap. On the days when there was a meet in the vicinity of Osberton he insisted on being taken, where, dressed in hunting costume and suitably mounted, he was able to enjoy the society and sounds of the chase and, indeed, follow the hounds by means of a leading rein attached to his groom's horse. His son, Francis, shared his father's enthusiasm for the hunt and was able to keep him up to date on all matters concerning it. Though denied a more active role, he relished the company of those who were able to ride and in the whole atmosphere of the hunt. It was written of him, "At a Yorkshire hound show, at Smithfield cattle show, in the yard at Tattersall's, in the paddock at Epsom, riding down Rotten Row, or even going to meet hounds, the neat sportsmanlike figure of the Osberton squire was almost to the last familiar enough."[9]

Although this photograph was taken some years after George Savile Foljambe's death, the sound and sight of the hounds outside Osberton Hall were familiar in his time too. From his earliest years he was an enthusiastic follower of the hunt and, until blindness struck, was master of the Grove Hunt. Even then, it was his delight to attend a meet and follow its progress, as far as possible, by means of a leading rein attached to his groom's horse.

Black as 1845 seemed, it had one brighter moment for in that year Mr. Foljambe re-married. His second wife was a widow, Lady Selina Milton. In the following year their son, Cecil, was born and there were other children of the marriage. Doubtless the sound and chatter of his children brought some happiness to the blind squire as did his continued interest in and enjoyment of his home and its surroundings. He was often at the Home Farm where he had flocks of Southdown and Leicester sheep as well as a herd of shorthorn cattle, some of which were prizewinners at the leading agricultural shows. Another of his favourite haunts was the gardens of the hall. These have been described as amongst the finest in the county, "sweet and luxuriant, and not mere hard and scentless works of art."[10] Here such flowers as the heliotrope perfumed the air; a delight for the nose even if the eye could not appreciate their beauty.

Life still had more for Mr. Foljambe than talking about hounds and taking his ease in his garden. He had already provided a church on his estate: now, towards the end of his life, he was told of the need for another. This was at nearby Worksop, a town that was growing in extent and population and where the Priory Church was the only Anglican place of worship. In 1862, at a public meeting, a committee was appointed to consider ways and means of increasing that provision. They were encouraged by the immediate offer from Mr. Foljambe of £1,000, half to go towards the building costs, the rest to the endowment. His only proviso was that the new church should be built on the west side of the town. He later increased his donation to £3,000 to the endowment fund and £1,000 towards building costs. This made him, by far, the most generous benefactor of the new church which, it was decided was to be known as St. John's, the same dedication as the church he had built at Scofton some thirty five years previously. Building work complete, the church was consecrated by the Archbishop of York on the 9th August, 1869. Prominent among those present were Mr. Foljambe, his wife Lady Milton and his eldest son, Mr. F.J. S. Foljambe who was then Member of Parliament for Bassetlaw.

Happy as the day undoubtedly was, in retrospect it was tinged with sadness as it was one of the last occasions when many Worksop people saw the "blind squire." He died on the 18th December of the same year. Before the funeral service, a long procession of carriages and people on foot moved from Osberton Hall to the church at Scofton, which was packed with a gathering of family, friends and those who had lived and worked on the estate. After due tribute had been paid, the coffin was borne to the vault by six of his oldest workmen and placed beside those of his first wife, his mother and two of his children. In Worksop a public subscription was opened to provide a fitting memorial to so benevolent a neighbour and as a result a stone reredos was installed in the chancel of St. John's church. Memory is short and fashions change and this was taken out and replaced in 1932. Now the building itself stands in memory of its principal benefactor, a man who typified throughout his life all that was best in the image of a fine old English gentleman.

Notes and References

1. The Nottingham Review, 18 April, 1851.
2. Country Life, 2 March, 1978. N. Pevsner. The Buildings of Nottinghamshire, 1979.
3. The Nottingham Daily Guardian, 28 December, 1869.
4. N. Pevsner. The Buildings of Nottinghamshire.
5. T. Parkinson in the Retford and Gainsborough Times, 18 November, 1887.
6. The Nottingham Review, 26 May, 1868.
7. Ibid. 8 June, 1848.
8. Ibid.
9. The Field, quoted in the Nottingham Daily Guardian, 28 December, 1869.
10. Leonard Jacks. The Great Houses of Nottinghamshire and the County Families. 1881.

PICTURE SUPPLEMENT, 6
THE PRINCE OF WALES AT WORKSOP.

THE PRINCE INSPECTING THE YEOMANRY AND VOLUNTEER CORPS AT WORKSOP.

This picture appeared in the Illustrated Times of the 26th October, 1861 and shows the reception of the Prince of Wales on his arrival at Worksop station prior to his visit to the Duke and Duchess of Newcastle at Clumber. Duty was combined with pleasure for the Prince, the former taking him to Shireoaks where he laid the foundation stone of the church and spent half an hour examining the surface installations at the colliery, declining an invitation to descend to the coal face.

Before the general use of photography, a deft hand with a pencil was a necessary skill for anyone wanting to illustrate such a scene as this. Within a few minutes, the mounted procession would be on its way to Clumber and the crowd have dispersed. Details of the buildings could then be added though as for the rest, anything not already set down would depend on the artist's memory.

There is a Tavern in the Town.

No one living in 19th century Worksop had far to walk to the nearest public house. They clustered around the market place and dotted almost every street in the town. At least sixty of them, they varied in size from the humble beerhouse to the large posting establishment. All supplied refreshment: most also provided the venues for a wide variety of activities: social, business, sporting, political, welfare and even occasionally medical. Much that happened in the town centred on the inn. Although they were often condemned as the sources of drunkenness and unruliness, such criticisms should be weighed against the many benefits that they provided.

This photograph of the Black Swan was taken at the end of November, 1966 just two days before it closed. Quite small and unpretentious, it was a "local," drawing its custom from the neighbouring streets of the Marecroft area.

Old as many of them looked, little is known of the history of Worksop's public houses and inns. An inn called the Angel changed ownership in 1613 [1] while an early account of the George tells that it was destroyed by fire in 1653, it, "having been tyme out of minde a victualling house." It was soon rebuilt [2] and retained its 17th century appearance until it was closed in 1909. Architecturally the Old Ship may have been of even greater antiquity though it is not known if it had always been an inn. Two others of similar date are known because trade tokens have been found bearing their names. These were the Apothecaries' Arms and the Grocers' Arms. [3] There are also occasional 18th century references to other inns in the town. These mention the Unicorn, the

Wheatsheaf , the Plumbers' Arms and the Red Lion. The latter was certainly in existence in 1745 for a meeting was held there on the 27th June to find out how many townsmen, "of no lawful calling," were eligible to be levied into the army.

Later, in 1789, it was scathingly condemned by Colonel John Byng, "where we soon enter'd the Red Lion, a paltry looking inn, taking possession of a poor parlour, and ordinary supper, ... Nothing can have been nastier than our inn at Worksop: with ill cooking, stinking feather beds, and a conceited fool of a landlady:....."[4]

Obviously there were more public houses than these few and a list published in 1822 [5] which names four inns and seventeen taverns and public houses, though still incomplete, presents a truer picture. At that date the differences between inns and other types of hostelries was still marked. The former were usually larger and offered travellers both accommodation and posting facilities: the others were often more modest establishments and while some provided similar services to the inn, they did not have to. Many were simply beer houses. By the 1870's some of these distinctions had begun to blur and the word hotel was replacing the older title of inn. Thus in Worksop the infamous Red Lion Inn of 1789 became the much praised Lion Hotel and the Bull Inn became the Royal Hotel. Of the other two inns mentioned in the 1822 list, the Crown was demolished to make way for the building of the Town Hall and the George was in decline, soon, in 1909, to be declared redundant and closed. This was sad because early in the century the George was considered by many to be the principal inn of the town. Between 1802 and 1804 it was repaired throughout, its stock of post horses was doubled and its landlord, Mr. Jeremiah Mallatratt, boasted of, "A good Larder, choice Wines and good Beds."[6]

However, seventy years later, the Lion was unquestionably the principal house in the town. Behind its neat and pleasing Georgian facade were three private sitting rooms, twenty two bedrooms, two large rooms used as market and dining rooms, commercial and coffee rooms, a bar, a tap room, a billiard room, kitchens, pantries and cellars. Facing the yard at the back was stabling for thirty six horses, coach houses, wash houses and other outbuildings. With such a range of accommodation and amenities it is unlikely that any other establishment in the district could rival it. That it deserved its pre-eminence can be judged from the testimony of a visitor. "For instance, I am writing these lines in a cosy sitting room of that most comfortable of inns or hotels, the Lion."[7] Largely responsible for this reputation was Mr. R.M. Morris who began the 1870's as a yearly tenant paying £125 rent but who, in 1875, bought the hotel for £3,600. After increasing the accommodation to what has just been mentioned he was unfortunately forced to sell it three years later. At this second sale the price was £4,500 plus extra for furniture and fittings. The new owner was the firm of Smith and Nephew, one of the town's breweries soon, in 1881, to amalgamate with the Priorwell Brewery to form the Worksop and Retford Brewery Company. No one can doubt the soundness of the purchase. The Lion continued to be the venue for the cream of the town's social occasions as well as providing appropriate accommodation for the tourist and the business man. The hotel's own publicity made this quite clear. "The hotel is largely used by families from all parts, and from commercial gentlemen visiting the town, and the market ordinary is attended by all the principal agriculturalists in the neighbourhood."[8]

The smaller establishments were essentially places for drinking and their layout was planned for that purpose. The Unicorn's central doorway opened into a tap room that ran the width of the building while behind it was a tiny snug, a small bar in a passageway and a kitchen. When occasion demanded however, the Unicorn could provide a meal such as when the employees of local builder Mr. Sidney Tuten had their annual dinner. About thirty sat down to, "a most ample spread provided by the host and hostess."[9] Perhaps one of the upstairs rooms was used when catering for such numbers. Accommodation was no more commodious at the Manton Inn. A central bar served both tap and smoke rooms as well as a small snug. Quarry tiles covered the floor and seating was on hard backed chairs.

Another "local," the Fox on Lowtown Street, survived a little longer than the Black Swan. It was not until 1973 that it was demolished, together with the adjacent cottages. All were very old buildings and could have been standing on the foundations of even earlier ones. The Fox looks as if it might originally have had a thatched roof.

Such conditions seemed typical of the smaller houses and were obviously accepted as, even in warm weather, there was little inducement to drink out of doors. Mostly facing the street, hemmed in by neighbouring property and backed by an assortment of outbuildings where the atmosphere was redolent of the farm yard, few inns had the space to provide a pleasant outside area. Just about every inn had its own stable. The Marquis of Granby had two together with four loose boxes while larger establishments such as the Station Hotel had a coach house as well. Pig sties were usual features of inn yards and the New Inn on Lead Hill also had a cow house. Other buildings often included wash houses, coal houses, sheds and the toilet facilities. By 1882, when rough plans were drawn of some of the inns belonging to the newly formed Worksop and Retford Brewery Company, a number very clearly had water closets though it is not apparent that all were so equipped. One isn't marked at the Oddfellows Arms though an ash pit is indicated as is a pump. The omission of a W.C. may have been the fault of the draughtsman or it could be that the necessary piped water supply had not yet been taken so far up Netherton Road. However comfortless, even primitive, the ordinary public house may sound to the modern ear it suffered no lack of patronage a hundred or so years ago. After a working day that was often long and arduous, the tap room fire was warmly inviting, the company convivial and the beer both cheap and strong. For many this seemed much preferable to a damp, cold cottage where the plight of a large family was all too obvious. After the rigours of the day most men were content to sit, drink their nightly pint and talk among themselves. Recalling such a scene in the early years of the last century, a lady who grew up in an inn where her father was landlord wrote, "..... conversation was regarded as No. 1 on the list of entertainments. Men loved to relate the happenings in the olden days and recall their prowess in the field of sport. They were proud of their strength, and it was quite usual with sleeves rolled up exhibiting their biceps, and having a bet on the breadth of chest, how much weight they could lift and many other feats of strength."[10] For those wanting something more active to do, choice was limited. Although customers at the Lion and Royal could enjoy a game of billiards, cards and dominoes were the usual fare in the smaller houses.

The Old Ship Inn, facing the Market Place, was the best known of all Worksop's hostelries. This old photograph, taken around 1900, shows it hemmed in between Schofield's grocery shop and the White Hart Inn. Following the demolition of the shop, the Old Ship was extended to its present size. It would be interesting to know the reason for its illuminated decorations. The absence of the national flag and the monarch's monogram suggests that it wasn't a royal occasion.

The Greyhound was a large, town centre inn that stood on the Market Place. As well as catering for local custom, it also hoped to attract visitors and passing trade. The extensive outbuildings at the back provided accommodation for horses and carriages. The Greyhound was a popular venue for meetings, dinners and entertainments while, in summer, it arranged horse drawn coach trips round the Dukeries.

Unfortunately not every night at the inn was as tranquil as has just been described. There was drunkenness, there were arguments: neither unruliness nor unpleasantness was unknown. This must be remembered when considering the social influence of the public house in the second half of the 19th century. As indeed must the much more favourable fact that most meetings that were not to do with church or civic affairs were held at an inn. Thus it was that at a meeting in 1866 at the Golden Ball that the Worksop Co-operative Society was formed while the Chamber of Trade was inaugurated at a meeting at the Lion in 1875. Just about every inn appeared to have a suitable room for such gatherings. Small as it was, the Newcastle Arms had a large club room at the back while the White Horse on Abbey Street boasted rooms capable of holding any number between ten and two hundred. The Golden Ball was also the venue for a meeting in 1875 when Mr. Thomas Graham, a Canadian Government Commissioner, spoke about his country to a "fair attendance" of people considering emigration. In the same year the Worksop Cricket Club discussed their sad plight of having no ground at their annual general meeting at the Bull Commercial Hotel. These were single occasions but many organisations held their regular week by week meetings at a convenient inn while clubs, societies, work mates and almost every group of people with mutual interests gathered at an inn for their annual dinner.

The annual dinner enjoyed its heyday in late Victorian times. Whether the participants were of the highest or the humblest, strict protocol was followed. After the meal, often appetisingly described in the local paper in such terms as "well loaded tables of creature comforts," a "most excellent repast," or "a most substantial and excellent spread," a chairman and vice chairman were elected. Thus when the Worksop Post Office held its annual supper in 1878 at the Royal Hotel, Mr. Thomas Parkinson, Postmaster, was elected to the chair and Mr. J.R. Pennington, the sub-postmaster, to the vice chair.[11] Then followed a series of speeches and toasts, often proposed at length though invariably drunk with enthusiasm. This part of the evening might be interspersed with songs if visiting artists were present and the proceedings generally ended with singing.

Now modernised in appearance and re-named the Carlton Tavern, the Railway Inn was conveniently sited for users of the nearby station and workers at the Clinton maltkilns. Until the coming of motor vehicles, good stabling was as essential to attract travelling custom as is a car park nowadays.

Not surprisingly a number of organisations chose the Lion for their dinners. During 1875 the employees of the Manchester, Sheffield and Lincolnshire Railway, the Clumber Troop of the Sherwood Rangers Yeomanry, the local Rifle Volunteers and the Worksop Labourers' Friend Society were among groups who enjoyed "Mr.and Mrs. Morris's excellent dinners." Other larger establishments such as the George, the Golden Ball, the Ship and the Station Hotel were well patronised though some of the more modest houses also catered. Friendly Societies dined at the Blue Bell, the Wheatsheaf and the Prior Well Inn, pig clubs at the Boundary and the Travellers' Rest while Mr. Barlow's Shoe Club spent an "Enjoyable evening" at the French Horn. In addition to providing dinners for special occasions, many of Worksop's inns boasted their ability to cater for all comers at virtually any time. The Old Bull Inn could, "provide every kind of Refreshment, on the Shortest Notice," while "beef steaks any hour of the day" could be tasted at the White Hart. Both the Blue Bell Inn and the Boundary Inn advertised "Chops, Tea and Coffee on the Shortest Notice" and the Bull Inn invited custom to its "Excellent Market Dinners." Such a list[12] is not complete; it simply serves as a sample of what was available.

Among the most regular users of large rooms of some of Worksop's inns of late Victorian times were the town's Friendly Societies. Here they met to collect subscriptions and disburse benefits, here they sat down to their annual dinners and enjoyed other social occasions. There were at least six societies in the town[13] and two of them were named after the inns that they made their headquarters. These were the Wheatsheaf Friendly Society and the Golden Ball Friendly Society. In the days before unemployment benefit and other means of social security, the Friendly Societies were a way for the prudent to make provision should illness or other adversity strike. One local advocate of the movement wrote, "It (the Friendly Society) has made the members comfortable in sickness, and kept their spirits buoyant and free, by the assurance that the money they received was their own."[14] Not surprisingly support was good. Total membership of the Worksop lodges in the 1870's hovered around five hundred and the town would see their strength on their annual Whitsuntide processions. On these occasions, members assembled at their own club rooms and, at 11 o'clock, marched to the Priory Church, led by a band. After the service the Societies returned to their inns for dinner. By 1875 this custom was beginning to decline as only three Societies took part. Even so it would cause quite a stir in the streets. The Golden Ball Friendly Society, some two hundred and twenty strong, was headed by the Worksop Brass Band as it marched to and from the church. The Harthill Band led the one hundred and five members of the Wheatsheaf Friendly Society while the Shireoaks Band preceded the one hundred and sixty members of the Abbey Society from their club room to the church and afterwards to the Old Ship Inn for their dinner.

With regular meetings, usually fortnightly, annual dinners and other social events to cater for, an inn that housed a Friendly Society was virtually guaranteed much extra custom. Additionally, by the 1870's the Societies were generally respected, they were financially sound and had an air of solidity and permanence about them. Although most of their members counted their weekly wage in shillings and pence, the Societies' funds ran to hundreds and sometimes thousands of pounds. In 1875 the accumulated fund of the Golden Ball Society almost totalled £2,000. This was made up of twelve cottages, £400 on mortgage, £100 in the bank and £50 "in the Box", presumably cash in hand for current disbursements. During the past year the Society had paid out £236 - 3 - 0d (£236.15) in sickness benefits and £56 to the families of members who had died.[15] The fact that such a Society used one particular inn would do much for the reputation of the house and doubtless attract more custom to its bars.

Similarly fortunate in supplementing their regular patronage were the inns used as bases by the local carriers. Although the railways had replaced the horse drawn coach as a means of long distance travel, there was still a need for a road link between Worksop and its neighbouring towns and villages. This was supplied by the carrier's cart. Usually a four wheeled wagonette with a form along each side for seating and a tarpaulin cover in wet weather, it was pulled along the uneven and often unmade country roads at two or three miles an hour. On reaching Worksop the cart was left outside an inn and the horse put into a stable while the passengers went about their business and the driver carried out his commissions and errands. In the 1880's six Worksop inns were used by twenty two carriers who served thirty places. Most distant were Sheffield, Chesterfield and Doncaster: closest were Gateford and Shireoaks. The White Hart on Bridge Street was the most popular with the carriers as seven used it as their base, next was the French Horn with six while the Wheatsheaf was favoured by five. Two left their carts at the Old Ship and one at the Queen's Head and the Golden Ball.

J.T. Shardlow of the Portland Works on Clarence Road was a manufacturer of mineral and aerated waters, widely sold in public houses and shops in Worksop and district. Here one of the firm's horses and drays has been decked out for a special occasion, probably a procession that was held on Empire Day in the early years of the 20th century. Clearly the Worksop and Retford Brewery Company acted as agent for the sale of Shardlow's products. (Picture by permission of The Bassetlaw Museum).

Not surprisingly five of the inns called at by the carriers were either adjacent to or within a short walk of the market place though neither of Worksop's principal houses, the Lion and the Royal, were used in spite of their convenient location. Perhaps their proprietors preferred to see their yards filled with the farmers' dog carts and their stables with somewhat superior horse flesh to the carrier's humble nag. The Lion, too, had several vehicles of its own, one of which, a horse drawn omnibus, ran a regular service between the station and the hotel, meeting every train. The others were available for private hire, sometimes carrying distinguished passengers. In April of 1878 carriages from the Lion took the Duchess of Newcastle, her children and her mother from the station to Clumber while in June of the same year Mr. Gladstone was similarly conveyed.[16]

Busiest time in the Lion's stables and in those of several other Worksop inns was the summer when visitors flocked to the town. The main attraction was the Dukeries and Sherwood Forest. The ducal parks were then in their prime, immaculately maintained by large staffs of workmen, the Forest was virtually unspoilt while Edwinstowe and Ollerton had an air of picturesque rural charm. All these delights could be enjoyed in the course of a twenty four mile drive, easily accomplished in the warmest hours of a summer's day. Permission to enter the parks of Clumber, Thoresby and Welbeck on specified days and proceed along a pre-determined route was granted to a number of people. They formed The Dukeries Posting Proprietors' Association and proudly advertised that they held keys and passes to the ducal parks "by the kindness of the several noble owners." Among the Worksop inns enjoying this privilege were the Lion, Royal, Station and Wheatsheaf. Most visitors making the trip came into the town by train and on the days of the week when the parks were open, Tuesdays, Thursdays and Saturdays, the station yard was packed with a variety of horse drawn vehicles ranging from the dog cart to the brake carrying twenty or more passengers. The usual procedure for those travelling with members of the Association was to be first taken to the appropriate inn for a late breakfast. The tour followed and the people were then brought back to their inn for another meal before making their way to the station.

The popularity of these trips was considerable and continued into the 20th century. "During the past week Worksop has received a large number of visitors," and, "Everyday brings visitors to Worksop and the Dukeries," reported the local paper[17] though a later comment that "these visitors do not help the trade of the town much" would hardly have been echoed by the innkeepers who belonged to the Posting Proprietors' Association. Mr. Cater of the Station Hotel certainly would not have complained when arranging for eighty four Huddersfield clerks and warehousemen with their wives and sweethearts to make the tour. The day went well as the convoy of eleven carriages made its way through "the beautiful sylvan scenery" and although the party dined at Edwinstowe, they would doubtless do full justice to the "substantial" tea provided for them on their return. After tea they, "enjoyed themselves as excursionists only can do, singing, etc., until the train arrived which was to take them back into Yorkshire."[18] Another group to choose the Station Hotel were thirty non-commissioned officers of the Sheffield Volunteer Engineers. "After an interval to recruit the inner man, " they went on their tour. "They spent a capital day, and in the evening sat down to a capital dinner provided by Mrs. Neale, returning to Sheffield by the 11.55 train midnight."[19] It is extremely unlikely that thirty N.C.O's would spend a whole evening at an inn without sampling the contents of the cellar and all innkeepers involved in the "tripping traffic" would anticipate a considerable increase in the demand for their beer in addition to the profits of catering and posting.

Sport is often associated with inns. It is discussed at the bars and sporting activities are often arranged or promoted by inns. This was certainly so a hundred or more years ago in Worksop though a great deal of information has not yet come to light about it. As early as 1850 William Wilson, landlord of the New Blue Bell Inn on Norfolk Street, made it known that he was a member of the Worksop Cricket Club and that he was prepared to lend out bats and balls "on reasonable terms."[20] A possible rival was the White Hart, described in an advertisement as "The Cricketers' House." While a cricketing landlord would attract both players and followers of the game and thereby encourage trade, one local inn was closed because of its involvement with sport. This was the Plough at Gateford. For many years it had been used as a training centre by athletes from South Yorkshire, most coming from the Sheffield area but some from as far afield as Barnsley and Huddersfield. Their presence was not welcome, "to ladies and gentlemen living near, who were hardly able to put their heads out of doors without encountering on the footpath men in scanty costume, ..."[21] When the lease expired in 1878 the owner refused to renew it to the landlord nor let the property be again utilised as an inn.

The Crown Inn, just off Sandy Lane, was similarly used and it could be that the athletes moved there after the closure of the Plough. Unfortunately they did not enjoy a reputation for good sportsmanship and tradition has it that the men ran either to the backers' or the bookies' orders and that their races were invariably fixed.[22] It is to be hoped that fair play was more apparent in late December of 1874 when the Wilcocks Great All England 180 yards Novice Handicap was held on the grounds of the George Inn. Mr. Wilcocks was the owner of the grounds which were at the back of the inn and were part of the Buslings, the large swathe of land that stretched between the east side of Bridge Street and the Priory Church. Earlier in the century the George's land had covered one hundred and sixty acres and was farmed.[23] In spite of the wintry weather the Novice Handicap proved a popular fixture and was watched by a crowd of about five hundred. Rabbit coursing was also held on the George's ground and attracted large attendances. At one meeting in 1878 the first prize was £5, the second £1 and the third 10 shillings (50p). As the newspaper report concluded," it is rather singular that almost all the favourites were defeated in the first round,"[24] it could perhaps be adduced that not everyone was perfectly satisfied with the probity of the sport. Completely above reproach were the sporting associations of the Bull. In 1875 it hosted the Annual General Meeting of the Worksop Cricket Club while in the next decade, catering for what was to be one of the most popular participatory sports, it provided a room for a cyclists' touring club house. Later in the century another sport with a strong local following was based at two of Worksop's inns. The Golden Ball was the head-quarters of the Worksop United Angling Association while members of the Grafton Angling Association transacted business at the inn of that name.

Although political matters were a regular and popular subject of discussion in most of Worksop's inns, they do not appear to have played much of a part in the political life of the town. This was no doubt because both the Conservatives and Liberals had their own club rooms where they would meet both formally and socially. An exception to this was at election times when, at the bye-election of 1876 inns were used by both parties as headquarters, the Conservatives at the Lion and the Liberals at the Bull.

For a time, as well as refreshment, justice was also dispensed at one of the town's inns for until the building of the Corn Exchange in 1851, the Magistrates' Court was held at the George. The court room was on the first floor and it remained intact until the inn was closed. The magistrates' bench was in the large bay that overhung the street and there was also a dock, a witness box, a solicitors' table and public seats. Entrance was by a door in a side passage, appropriately known as Justices' Yard.[25]

Across at the Lion a much older court still met annually. This was the Court Leet, a relic of medieval times held by the Lord of the Manor or his steward, at which matters connected with land usage and local administration were settled. Before the reforms of the first half of the 19th century, the Court Leet was the unit of local government in towns that had not been granted borough status. This was so at Worksop so perhaps there was an excuse for its continuance even though real authority had passed to the Local Board of Health. On the 16th May, 1878 the Court duly assembled under the presidency of Mr. H.S. Hodding, steward of the Lord of the Manor. A jury of twenty four was impanelled and business transacted. This consisted of the appointment of officials; some useful such as the inspector of meat, fish and bread and the town crier and some archaic such as the pinder and the taster of beer. Nuisances about the town were reported and a particularly noisome sewer in Westgate was condemned. That done, the jury and their friends dined together and spent a pleasant evening.[26]

Less convivial though more necessary than the Court Leet, inquests were also held at inns. Following the death of Francis Wesley while at work at Tranter's brickyard an inquest was held at the Crown Inn.[27] After John Bedford was killed at Shireoaks Colliery the deputy coroner examined the circumstances of his death at the Boundary Inn. Bedford was a trammer and had attempted to take a tub loaded with eight hundredweight of coal down a 1 in 6 incline though he had been warned not to. He tried to steady the tub by placing his back against its front but was knocked down and run over. A verdict of accidental death was returned.[28] Mr. Whitehead, a commercial traveller, was more fortunate. Sustaining injuries after being thrown from his pony and trap somewhere between Whitwell and Worksop he was immediately taken to the Lion where he received attention from Dr. Lloyd.[29] As Worksop had no hospital until 1901 it is unlikely that he was the only accident victim to be given medical treatment at an inn.

Much has been said about money wasted at inns but little about money saved in them. This latter comment certainly applied to the George in the early years of the 19th century as the Worksop Savings Bank was founded there in 1817 and began business in the following year. Although early publicity encouraged potential members with the thought, "If you will save with the bank one shilling a week for seven years you will then have £20, which will buy you a cow, furnish your cottage and apprentice your son, " it is unlikely that custom was brisk as the bank was only open for two hours a week. In 1826 when the landlord's rent was increased from £60 to £85 a year, the bank agreed to raise the annual payment for its room from two guineas to three. The bank remained at the George until 1844 when it moved to its own premises.[30]

Inns have always been places for buying and selling whether it be the private bargain or more public business. In particular auctions were often held there. The Lion was regularly used, as in early 1875 when Mr. Frank Sissons held his annual sale of timber. Forty lots were sold for almost £5,000 and, business done, all sat down to one of Mrs. Morris's "splendid dinners."[31] Another annual business occasion also took place at the Lion. This was the Duke of Portland's "Pay Day." On the 26th March, 1878 all local tradesmen who had dealings with the Duke during the previous year presented their accounts and received payment.[32] The report does not say whether they received refreshment as well as cash though it is unlikely that they went away with their thirst unslaked.

More importantly than the many and various functions that have been mentioned, the inn was firstly and foremostly a place of warmth, hospitality and conviviality. This was well exemplified in 1893 when Mr. F.L. Green of the Lion revived an old custom of bygone days by inviting regular patrons of the market ordinary to a free new year champagne dinner. Doubtless those partaking felt a glow of satisfaction, that the Lion was a fine house and that Worksop was well served by its principal inn. Even allowing for the abuse made of their facilities, the drunkenness and the petty crime, the unruliness and degradation that sprang from them, all the town's inns could in part share in the Lion's reputation. They filled a real social need, they provided accommodation for business and civic functions and amenities for a host of organisations and activities that brightened the prospect and made more bearable the trials of a hard life.

Notes and References

1. Nottinghamshire County Records .. .. of the Seventeenth Century. Compiled by H.H. Copnall. 1915.
2. Quarter Session Minute Book.
3. Robert White. Worksop, the Dukery and Sherwood Forest. 1875.
4. Colonel John Byng. The Torrington Diaries.
5. London and Provincial Directory. Pigot.
6. Alan W. Mallatratt. The Mallatratts of Mansfield.
7. The Retford and Gainsborough Times. 6 September, 1878.
8. Ibid.
9. Ibid. 4 September, 1875.
10. Miss May Lowe. Worksop Guardian: date unknown.
11. The Retford and Gainsborough Times. 8 February, 1878.
12. R. White. The Visitors' Hand-book to Worksop.
13. The Retford and Gainsborough Times. 20 November, 1875.
14. C. Thomson. The Autobiography of an Artisan.
15. The Retford and Gainsborough Times. 22 May, 1875,
16. Ibid. 14 June, 1878.
17. Ibid. 21 June and 15 July, 1881.
18. Ibid. 15 July, 1876.
19. Ibid. 12 July, 1878.
20. An advertisement in The Visitors' Hand-book to Worksop. R. White. 1850.
21. The Retford and Gainsborough Times. 30 March, 1878.
22. Undated cutting from the Worksop Guardian.
23. Alan W. Mallatratt. The Mallatratts of Mansfield. 1976.
24. The Retford and Gainsborough Times. 9 February, 1878,
25. Undated cutting from the Worksop Guardian of an article by Edwin Topham.
26. The Retford and Gainsborough Times. 24 May, 1878.
27. Ibid. 31 May, 1878.
28. Ibid. 9 October, 1875.
29. Ibid. 10 June, 1879.
30. Undated cutting from the Worksop Guardian.
31. The Retford and Gainsborough Times. 6 March, 1875
32. Ibid. 30 March, 1878.

"It's The Poor What Gets the Blame."
Law and Order in Worksop in 1875.

If 1875 was a typical year, and evidence suggests that it was, then Superintendent James Blaisdale could feel well content with his appointment as officer in charge of the police in Worksop. Serious crime was rare: the great majority of cases that came before the magistrates were petty and though there was an unruly element in the town it was chiefly apparent after the public houses had closed. Main occupants of the four cells of the brick built [1] Police Station on Potter Street were drunks. Little happened that the superintendent, his two sergeants and eleven constables could not handle. That their work was appreciated was apparent after Mr. F. J. Boaler, a member of the Board of Guardians of the Poor Law Union, criticised them at a meeting. He said, "It was perfectly absurd to put the matter (of finding a missing person) in the hands of the Worksop police; ..... They wore the clothes and bright buttons and received the pay, but that was about all."[2]

Mr. Boaler was severely taken to task in the local paper where it was pointed out that there had only been one case of serious crime in the past five years[3] and he was contradicted at the Board's next meeting by its chairman, the Revd. Mr.Hawley, Vicar of Worksop, who said that, "Worksop had at the present time a better set of men than he had ever known in the parish."[4]

To deal with those who were apprehended by the police, the local Petty Sessions or Magistrates' Court was held fortnightly though additional sittings could be arranged if necessary. Ten magistrates were appointed to the local bench but, on occasions, they were joined by some from outside the district.

One such visitor was Colonel Henry Eyre of Rampton Manor who would normally

H. V. MACHIN, Esq.

It was men such as Henry Vessey Machin of Gateford Hill who occupied the bench at Worksop's magistrates' court during the 19th century. Almost without exception the local justices of the peace were members of the landed gentry. Only towards the end of the century were they joined by professional men. Even Joseph Garside, Worksop's most influential and richest man, was denied a place on the bench.

officiate at Retford. With one exception the Worksop bench was solidly representative of the landed interest, embracing the gentry, the squirearchy and the country gentleman. The one exception was Mr. Charles Tylden Wright, a distinguished mining engineer and the Head Manager of Shireoaks Colliery. The other magistrates were Earl Manvers of Thoresby, Colonel Sir Thomas Woollaston White of Wallingwells, Mr. F.J.S. Foljambe of Osberton, Colonel S.W. Welfitt of Langwith, Mr. R.J. Ramsden of Carlton, Mr.H.V. Machin of Gateford, Mr. H. Beevor of Blyth, Mr. T.H.D. Bayley of Edwinstowe and Mr. G.W. Mason of Ranby.

Some of these magistrates were much more familiar figures at court than others. It was usual for two, three or four to be present though twice in 1875 there were six and once only one. Backbone of the Worksop bench was Colonel White, Mr. Beevor, Mr. Mason and Mr. Tylden Wright with fifteen or more appearances during the year, closely followed by Mr. Bayley who attended thirteen times. No other magistrate officiated on more than four occasions.

A complaint sometimes voiced about the magistrates was that none of them lived in the town, the nearest being Mr. Machin at Gateford and Mr. Tylden Wright at Shireoaks. The sad case of a woman severely beaten by her husband brought this question to the fore. She could not take out a summons against him as her injuries prevented her walking eight miles to the house of the nearest available magistrate. As at least half the bench lived less than eight miles away it must be assumed that they were away from home at the time of the woman's incident.

The Worksop Tradesmen's Association discussed the matter and suggested the names of three prominent townsmen who they thought would make suitable magistrates. Support came from the local paper [5] which agreed that these men should be appointed and the bench increased to fifteen or sixteen. At the same time it was very careful not to breathe any criticism of the existing magistrates. "Not that some new magistrates are needed because of the inability of those we have. I do not think there is a town anywhere where justice is so ably dealt out as at Worksop by the present list of magistrates."[6] Not surprisingly so small a ripple of agitation failed to bring about any immediate change. Worksop's magistrates continued to converge on the court house from the surrounding villages on horseback or in dog cart while poor townspeople who wanted their help had to struggle on foot to their country residences.

The columns of the local press[7] record in some detail the business of the magistrates' courts and glancing through these reports, the pattern of law breaking in the Worksop of 1875 soon becomes apparent. The majority of people who appeared before the bench were poor, some so poor that poverty may have pushed them beyond the law though most were there because of drunkenness and its effects. An analysis of the different cases that were dealt with in 1875 and the number of people charged with each reinforces the point that most offenders were unfortunate rather than criminals.

Offence	No. of Prosecutions
Drunkenness	42
Poaching	33
Assault	22
Theft	17
Non-vaccination of child (2 people)	17
Wilful damage	9
Breach of the peace	9
Causing an obstruction	8
Playing pitch and toss	7
Not having a dog licence	5
On licensed premises out of hours	4
Wife beating	3
Cruelty to animals	3
Firearms offences	2
Offences under the Master and Servant Act	2
Quarrels down the pit	2
Non-payment of rates	2
Failure to report foot and mouth disease	2
House breaking	2
Supplying drink out of hours	1
Using threats	1
Embezzlement	1
Chimney fire	1
Indecent assault	1
Sale of bad meat	1
Using a catapult	1
Travelling on railway without a ticket	1
Smoking in a railway carriage	1
Ticket of leave offence	1
Begging	1
Pickpocket	1
Non-payment of wages	1
Leaving family chargeable to the Poor Law Union	1
Trespassing with intent	2

On the evidence of these figures, and it must be stressed that they represent the number of cases reported in the local press, there was certainly no crime wave in Worksop. What there was, and this is in part suggested, was some unpleasantness, some unsavoury sights and some unruliness. Fortunately such incidents chiefly occurred late at night. "If anyone wants to be edified in an unpleasant manner, let him (the "Hers" had best not try) to take a turn round some of our streets after closing time on Saturday nights. Of course they would not see worse things in Worksop than are to be seen in any town of the same size and larger; but they would have an experience and go home wiser men."[8]

This was written by the Worksop correspondent of the Retford and Gainsborough Times and it was a subject that he mentioned regularly in his column. In view of the picture he paints the number of arrests for drunkenness seems small and it is likely that the police turned a blind eye to many offenders and only intervened if other people were inconvenienced, if fighting broke out or if property was damaged. While the Retford Times fulminated against the drunkard, "never in any one place have they (visitors to the town) seen so many drunken men .....never in any place have they observed so many drunken women,"[9] little was done to combat it. This is perhaps not too surprising as there were two large breweries in the town and over twenty working maltkilns. Too many peoples' livelihoods were involved in the production of beer to expect any great support for restricting its sale. Thus the temperance movement was not particularly strong in the town. There were two lodges of Good Templars, the Spread Eagle and the Hope of Worksop, and although their regular meetings were attended by members and friends, an evening of songs, recitations, exhortations and a cup of tea in a chapel schoolroom would not attract many from the bar of the nearby public house. At best, reports on these meetings spoke of a pretty good attendance,"[10] at worst of "but a thin attendance."[11]

Those apprehended by the police in the streets were usually charged with being drunk and disorderly or drunk and riotous. They were fined between five and fifteen shillings (25p and 75p), had to pay costs and, in default of payment, some of them were sentenced to ten or fourteen days in custody. After breaking a large pane of glass in Mr. Valentine's grocer's shop, George Green had to pay the usual five shilling fine (25p), costs and a further five shillings for damages. Failing payment he faced fourteen days in custody. More serious was being drunk and in charge of a vehicle. William Booth was in such a state while driving his horse and cart and was fined £1, plus costs. That the police were ready for any contingency was illustrated when, one Sunday night,

For a time during the first half of the 19th century, the Worksop magistrates' court met in the room that overhung the pavement of the George Inn on Bridge Street. The room was appropriately furnished with a bench for the justices, a dock for those facing trial, a witness box, solicitors' table and seats for the public. These remained in position long after the court had moved to more suitable premises.

a woman was drunk and incapable just as people were returning home from church. She was hastily put into a wheel barrow and trundled home by three policemen; two holding her, the third pushing. No charge was brought. Less easy to ignore were fights between parties of drunken men. One such fracas occurred in late October; "At half past eleven o'clock on Saturday night, there was enacted at the 'common end' a drunken row, in which it was not the actors' faults that someone in their party was not kicked to death. Fancy what a nice picture it would be to see a party of between twenty and thirty men charging one another like mad bulls, and when one of them kissed the dust half-a-score boots were 'into his ribs.' I never saw men work so hard, and do so much work in so short a time."[12] Five of the participants were charged with creating a disturbance, two did not appear at court, two were bound over on their own recognisances of £10 each while the fifth, obviously a man of some notoriety in the town with ten previous convictions, had to find two sureties of £20 each.

While the police were prepared to look the other way when the odd drunkard was staggering home and even to assist the drunk and incapable, they were much more

Poaching was one of the most common offences dealt with by the Worksop's magistrates' court during the second half of the 19th century. Gamekeepers were on constant lookout for poachers and tussles between the two factions were not unknown. This group of keepers posed for local photographer Amos Emblin. (Photograph by permission of the Bassetlaw Museum)

zealous in dealing with drunkenness in public houses. Chief scourge of the landlords who could not keep good order were Sergeants Gee and Hall, though the latter was unlucky on at least one occasion. He went into the Norfolk Arms where he saw a number of noisy and drunk men. Going upstairs he met several young women coming down. They were also drunk and using bad language. Entering the parlour he saw six or eight men who were drunk and the landlord, who was lying drunk on a sofa.

That such a large haul should come to nothing seems strange but the sergeant could not positively identify any of the accused when not in their cups and the case was dismissed.[13] A further example has rather a plaintive air to it, redolent of a Victorian ballad. Charles Kemp, landlord of the White Horse Inn, Abbey Street, was charged with permitting drunkenness as Sergeant Gee and P.C. Hayes found a man there who was drunk but quiet. It was stated that the man's son, a boy of ten, had been to the inn and asked Kemp not to let his father have any more drink. Kemp was fined £3, plus costs and his licence was endorsed.[14] Such prosecutions were worrying to the landlords and through the Licensed Victuallers' Association they presented a petition to the bench asking for more understanding by the police. They pointed out that a person could have become drunk at one place and then moved on to another without showing any visible signs of his condition. One more drink might make all the difference and it was the landlord of the second inn who was at risk of prosecution. The magistrates' attitude to this petition is not known: perhaps it was too delicate a subject on which to comment publicly.

They were less reticent at the Brewster Sessions of 1875 when Mr. J.B. George of Norfolk Street presented a memorial asking the magistrates not to grant any more licences and complaining about Saturday night drunkenness. Mr. Appleton, a solicitor representing the Licensed Victuallers' Association, described the memorial as cowardly and uncalled for and Colonel Woollaston White, the chairman of the sessions, administered the final snub. The bench had accepted the memorial, he said, but of course they would put their own value on it.[15] On the whole the magistrates were reasonably tolerant towards the landlords: at the same sessions, although complaints and objections were raised against two houses, their licences were renewed,[16] as were those of all the other inns in the town.

In spite of the newspaper's invective, the Good Templars' social evenings, Mr, George's memorial, the late night police patrols and the magistrates' fines, drunks continued to dominate the court sessions. Unhappily drunkenness sometimes led to other offences and it is likely that some of those charged with assault or causing a breach of the peace would never have been so involved had they not been drinking. William Thomas had been drinking in the New Inn on Lead Hill. His subsequent behaviour was described as disgraceful and his language as disgusting. He threw a newspaper onto the fire, followed it with another man's dinner and hit the landlady several times on the head with his hat. Later he knocked a candlestick out of her hand while striking at her with his fist. He was fined 21 shillings (£1.05) plus 19 shillings (95p) costs.[17] Samuel Bownes, said to be drunk and very quarrelsome, hit Mary Hudson in the mouth, making it bleed. This led to further trouble as Pamela Hudson was accused of assaulting Betsy Bownes and calling her insulting names. While fining Bownes 10 shillings (50p), the court dismissed the second case.[18] This seemed to be a usual procedure in a squabble between two families, where evidence was conflicting and blame difficult to apportion. For unprovoked assault the magistrates tended to be more severe. While having trouble with a drunken navvy who he was taking to the police station, a constable was attacked and kicked several times by Isaac Thomas of Shireoaks. The policeman released the navvy and arrested Thomas who was sentenced to one month's hard labour.[19] Patrick Feeley was given the same punishment after he had struck John Ward in the mouth and on the head with a stick.[20] Young offenders had the threat of corporal punishment as an inducement to better behaviour. At a Sunday School feast on Nicholson's field, George Wriglesworth attacked George Scrimshaw and kicked him four times. He had to pay 8 shillings (40p) costs and was told that he would be beaten with the rod if he appeared again.[21]

Worksop's most serious crime of 1875 began as a case of assault but assumed greater seriousness when the victim died. This resulted in Joseph Johnson, a nineteen year old pot hawker, being charged with feloniously killing and slaying Mrs. Jane Neale. The story was both sad and sordid. Mrs. Neale was walking towards Worksop when she was overtaken by a hawker's dray. She asked for and was given a ride, sitting beside Johnson who was driving. Another man was leading the horse. Mrs. Neale later alleged that Johnson made indecent approaches to her and she jumped from the dray in order to escape from him. Johnson stated that the wagon lurched, Mrs. Neale lost her balance and fell although he tried to hold her. Unfortunately Mrs. Neale landed awkwardly; breaking and badly tearing her right arm and cutting and bruising her face. A fortnight later lockjaw set in and she died.

Johnson appeared before the Worksop magistrates on several occasions and they heard much conflicting evidence on the case. Mrs. Neale's story was supported by members of her family while some of the hawkers tried to prove that the mishap was accidental. The bench committed Johnson to Nottingham Assizes, granting bail on two sureties of £100 each. While awaiting his trial, just one slender thread of hope might have comforted him. On the night of the incident, when brought before Mrs. Neale, lying injured in a Sandy Lane house, she failed to identify him as her assailant. In fact she picked out another hawker who was also present.[22]

In 1875 poaching was a widespread activity in the woods and fields around Worksop. For most this was probably a necessary way of supplementing the contents of the cooking pot though for some its main attraction may have been in the element of sport and risk with which it was spiced. A regular stream of men, apprehended by police and gamekeepers, appeared before the magistrates. Generally fines ranged between £1 and £2. A few were fined less: some with previous convictions considerably more. William Kemp was charged with using a dog to chase game in the Manor grounds. A gamekeeper saw two dogs chasing a hare and as Kemp was in the immediate vicinity he was charged. He denied the offence saying he was going for a walk with a friend but, having eleven previous convictions, he was fined £5 plus costs, with two months imprisonment with hard labour in default of payment. [23]

All forms of poaching were practised. James Smith was charged with using nets and ferrets on Featherbed Lane. He was fined £1-10-0d (£1.50) plus costs.[24] Four men, trespassing in Owday Wood, with two snap dogs and a terrier were each fined £1, plus costs[25] while John Starkey was charged with using a gun for the purpose of taking game. He was seen aiming at some pigeons but did not fire. He had a gun licence and although he somewhat plaintively asked in court, "What use is a licence if I can't shoot?" he was fined £1.2[26] Surreptitious fishing was also frowned upon. Three men who were apprehended while attempting to catch fish in the river near Lodge Farm were each fined 10 shillings (50p).[27] Perhaps the best poaching story of the year concerned William Wilson and Charles Webster who were charged with using a dog in pursuit of game. Joseph Curnall, gamekeeper to the Duke of Portland, watched the two men and the dog run a hare. He saw the men harden the dog on after the hare, noticed Wilson slip the dog and the dog chase the hare. Not so said Mr. Appleton, defending solicitor. The dog did not belong to the men. It was a stray that had followed them. They tied some string to its neck but it escaped and ran after the hare. It says much for the integrity of the Worksop bench that it accepted so specious a story in part mitigation of the men's act and only fined them 5 shillings (25p).[28]

The crime most severely punished by the Worksop bench was theft. This is hardly surprising as all the magistrates were men of property, brought up in the tradition that a person taking something that did not belong to him was worthy of condign, even heavy punishment. At the back of their minds would probably be memories of their younger days when thieves were still transported to penal settlements in Australia, In fact, this method of punishment had only been discontinued in 1857. Therefore though one month's hard labour may seem harsh for stealing a pork pie worth 1 shilling (5p)[29] the same misdemeanour could have been punished with seven years transportation less than fifty years earlier.

Imprisonment rather than fines was the usual way of dealing with those guilty of theft. The shortest sentence in 1875 was seven days for stealing a truss of hay [30] while the longest of six months was for stealing a gold watch and guard and some money.[31] Two others were referred to the Quarter Sessions, one of them giving Worksop its most exciting arrest of the year. In broad daylight a man entered the house of Mr. Frederick Bardwell at "Woodleigh" on Sparken Hill, He took two overcoats and silver cutlery worth £30. The alarm was given and a little later P.C. H.Lowery saw a suspicious character near the end of Pudding Lane further up Sparken Hill. The man, pulling a wooden stake from a hedge, prepared to defend himself but P.C. Lowery, in the words of the local paper, "a man of muscle and he can hit hard, and also with a will," drew his staff and attempted to make an arrest. A long fight ensued and ended with the thief, much belaboured and with a split head, being taken into custody.[32]

The most severe punishment was passed on a sixteen year old boy. William Morton worked for a chimney sweep and stole 2 shillings (10p). He was sent to prison for one month and after that to a reformatory for five years.[33] Earlier in the year he had been accused of stealing money from a house where he was working but had been dismissed with a caution because of the lack of evidence.[34] So heavy a sentence must surely have meant that he was no stranger to the magistrates.

Little need be said of most of the remaining cases that were brought before the bench. Just three merit a few words. The offences under the Vaccination Act could be almost equally divided between two men. Both the Revd. Mr. Oliver Beckerlegg and Mr. John Wood of Whitwell refused to have their children vaccinated. At approximately monthly intervals they were ordered to do so and at the same time fined for failing to comply with previous orders. By November Mr. Beckerlegg had paid £12-11-6d (£12.57) in fines and costs and Mr. Ward £11-5-6d (£11.27).[35]

Many Worksop families depended on the butchers' stalls in the market for their Sunday joint. As the hours passed the prices often fell and many a bargain was picked up in the glare of the naptha lamps just before closing time. Taking advantage of the customer's need and the indifferent light, Frederick Bell skewered some fresh pieces of fat to cuts of putrid meat. For offering for sale meat that was unfit for human consumption Bell was fined £20 plus £3-5-0d (£3.25) costs.[36]

A fairly new offence upon which Worksop's magistrates had to adjudicate concerned trouble down coal mines. Such incidents were not common as only two such cases, both assaults, were brought in 1875. Infrequent as they were, the bench had the man for the occasion and Mr. Tylden Wright was able to advise his fellows. When dealing with the first case, he said he was pleased the case had been brought, "for he was very anxious that these fights in the pit should be put an end to as they were attended with much danger."[37] The offending man was fined 15 shillings (75p) plus costs. The second offence was more serious and followed an argument between butties and trammers down Shireoaks pit. A trammer had just begun to fill a tub when another man hit him on the back with the shaft of a pick or a hammer. He fell and cut the back of his head. His attacker then belaboured him with his fists until he was bleeding badly and could hardly stand. A fine of £5 was imposed with two months imprisonment in default of payment.[38]

The only conclusion that can be drawn from the above evidence is that Worksop was a reasonably law abiding town. Most of its inhabitants went through 1875 without being the victim of any crime, without being the witness of any crime, without meeting any one in any way connected with any crime. Their only knowledge of law breaking would come from reading the reports of the Magistrates' Courts in the local paper. And yet many of these same people would probably complain bitterly about the state of the town for there was certainly unpleasantness on the streets, mischief and rowdyism were not uncommon and some were upset by sights and sounds that they found offensive. Much of the blame for this state of affairs was directed at the drunkard but he was not solely responsible. Gangs of boys tried to hustle pedestrians, especially ladies, and push them from the pavements. Others, armed with catapults were regarded as an even greater nuisance.[39] On one occasion twenty panes of glass were broken in the Abbey Infants' school room. After one lad had been brought before the magistrates, less was heard of catapults. The boys obviously deemed it wise to change their weapons and subsequently complaints were made about pea shooting.[40] In the Low Town area gangs wandered about at night, "knocking at doors, ringing bells and generally creating a riot and disturbance."[41] Bad language offended the sensitive ear and again children received a share of the blame. "I live in a line between two of our schools and am hurt considerably by the children stopping near my place and cursing, not at me but one another, in a horrible manner."[42] Doubtless the gentleman who made that complaint would both stop his ears and avert his eyes when passing a certain building at the bottom of Bridge Street. Delicacy did not permit the local paper to name it but referred to its inhabitants as, "a nest of bad characters" and "unclean inmates." It was no doubt a brothel. The occupants emerged one Sunday evening as people were passing on their way to church and one of them was heard to challenge any other woman to a fight for a bottle of gin.[43]

In the 1870's poverty and squalor dogged the days of many Worksop families. The former drove some to acts of petty crime in an attempt to alleviate their lots, the latter drove many to the inns for solace so that the degradation of their lives spilled out onto the streets. It was this, together with the boisterous and mischievous antics of a few gangs of boys, rather than the crime figures that offended some of the more better-off and vocal townspeople. The line from the popular chorus, "It's the poor what gets the blame," could certainly be quoted to summarise their attitude as they nodded their heads in agreement with the sentiments expressed in the local paper. Even pitch and toss, a popular and relatively harmless pastime, was castigated. "It's high time it was put a stop to, or rather checked."[44] The Worksop correspondent continued, "Go where you may on Sundays in the outskirts of the town, you come across parties thus enjoying themselves."

Perhaps it was the thought that the participants were enjoying themselves that rankled. Reading the lines and between the lines of the local paper there seemed a feeling of antipathy, a lack of understanding between some of the better off and some of the poorer people. This was a shame in a town where the crime rate was slight and where the more serious acts of nuisance were confined to the late evenings.

As 1875 ended, little did Superintendent Blaisdale and many of the townspeople think that before another year was out the comparative calm of Worksop would be shattered by the violence and destruction that took place on the voting day of a parliamentary bye-election. Many reasons caused this sudden and unexpected break down of law and order. One was surely a feeling by those who broke the windows, threw the bricks and battled with the police, that here was a chance for them to get a little of their own back on those who seemed so free with their blame and so lacking in their tolerance.

Notes and References

1. Recorded as such in 1860.
2. The Retford and Gainsborough Times. 26th June, 1875.
3. Ibid. 3 July, 1875.
4. Ibid. 10 July 1875.
5. Ibid. 12 June, 1875.
6. Ibid.
7. The Retford and Gainsborough Times.
8. Ibid. 1 May, 1875.
9. Ibid. 10 July, 1875.
10. Ibid. 1 May, 1875.
11. Ibid. 27 November, 1875.
12. 6 November, 1875.
13. 10 April, 1875.
14. 2 October, 1875
15. 11 September, 1875.
16. Ibid.
17. 31 July, 1875.
18. Ibid. 19 February, 1875.
19. Ibid. 27 November, 1875.
20. Ibid. 18 December, 1875.
21. Ibid. 14 August, 1875.
22. Ibid. 28 August, 1875.
23. Ibid. 31 July, 1875.
24. 8 May, 1875.
25. Ibid. 22 May, 1875.
26. Ibid. 31 July, 1875.
27. Ibid. 3 July, 1875.
28. Ibid. 11 September, 1875.
29. Ibid. 10 April, 1875.
30. Ibid. 11 September, 1875.
31. Ibid.
32. Ibid. 20 November, 1875.
33. Ibid. 5 June, 1875.
34. Ibid. 6 February, 1875.
35. Ibid. 13 November, 1875.
36. Ibid. 20 February, 1875.
37. Ibid. 17 April, 1875.
38. Ibid. 8 May, 1875.
39. Ibid. 13 February, 1875.
40. Ibid. 16 October, 1875.
41. Ibid.
42. Ibid. 20 November, 1875.
43. Ibid. 13 February, 1875.
44. Ibid. 5 June, 1875.

PICTURE SUPPLEMENT, 7
LIFE BOAT DAY AT WORKSOP.

Many in the town on Saturday, the 5th September, 1908 would have rubbed their eyes in dis-belief at the sight before them. Prominent in a procession that made its way along the main streets, carried on a trailer pulled by six horses that usually hauled the wagons of Smith's Albion Mills, was a life boat. Worksop was staging its first Life Boat Day, an event that was a popular way of raising money for what has always been a voluntary organisation. Almost as strange as the sight was the place of origin of the boat, as it was normally stationed at Tramore in County Waterford in Ireland. Worksop must have been just one stopping off place of a tour of such occasions.

Leaving the town centre, the procession headed along Newcastle Avenue to Beard's mill, where, with some difficulty, the boat was launched into the dam. There, to the delight of a crowd estimated at 4,000, various rescue techniques were demonstrated and local swimmers entertained with races and comic turns. Immediate proceeds totalled £62-10-0d (£62.50) to which would be added the contents of collection boxes that had been distributed about the town.

In Quest of Amos.
A Little Known Worksop Photographer.

Gedney Dyke is a small village in the Lincolnshire fens. It is about midway between Holbeach and Long Sutton though its nearest neighbour is Gedney, an older settlement whose magnificent late medieval church stands as a landmark in the rich, flat countryside. Sometime during 1856 Priscilla, wife of William Emblin, the village boot and shoe maker, gave birth to a baby boy. He was called Amos. An elder brother, Thomas, eight years his senior, was already one of the family and another boy, William, was born three years later. Shortly after his birth the three boys were motherless and in the care of Harriett Emblin who, at eighteen, was described in the 1861 census as housekeeper. Her precise position in the family is a little perplexing as she is further recorded as being daughter in law to William which suggests both early marriage and widowhood.

When King Edward VII and Queen Alexandra visited Welbeck in 1905, Amos Emblin was called from his shop to photograph the royal group. Two pictures are known of this occasion. This one shows the Queen and some of the ladies of the party. Amos Emblin seems to have had a free hand at Welbeck, photographing the Abbey and other buildings as well as groups of estate workers. (Photograph by permission of the Bassetlaw Museum).

Amos and his elder brother are described as scholars and their daily walk to their lessons would take them by footpath over the fields to Gedney where the building in which they tackled their studies still forms part of the village school. If the family was Anglican it would follow the same route to Sunday service; if non-conformist, there were two chapels in their own village, one Wesleyan the other United Methodist.

Ten years later, in 1871, the domestic situation had changed. William Emblin had re-married and Harriett had departed. Both Thomas and Amos had also left the family home and an elderly widow, Maria Harris, had taken up residence. Amos, at fifteen, had presumably gone away as prospects for work at Gedney Dyke were limited to the local farms, the handful of village shops and the tall, eight storey windmill that vied for prominence in the landscape with the tower of Gedney church. For those who aspired to anything different the only option was to seek it elsewhere and this young Amos must have done. Unfortunately, at the moment, it is not known where he went or what he did though the likelihood seems to be that he was employed in some sort of shop work.

Much could be written about this photograph by Amos Emblin. Suffice to say that it shows Smith's Albion Flour Mill, nearing completion. To the left of the mill, a malt kiln is just visible while to the right tree trunks in one of the town's timber yards are seasoning in the open air. In the foreground, a horse hauled narrow boat is making slow progress along the Chesterfield Canal. (Photograph from the Cecil Brown collection at Worksop Library).

Certainty returns with the 1881 census when Amos was in Worksop. He was twenty five, single and partner with Henry Hodges in a grocery and drapery business at 1, George Street. The property still stands. Henry Hodges was a year older than Amos Emblin and was to become well known in the musical life of the town. At different times he was organist at the Congregational chapel, St. John's church and for services at the Union Workhouse. The 1880's were significant years for Amos Emblin. They saw him marry, the birth of two of his children and set up in business on his own account. His wife, Minnie Sanderson, was a Worksop girl and three years his junior. Her family were market gardeners and their nursery covered three acres on Canal Road. Just before her marriage this was worked by her grandmother and mother, both widows, her younger brother and two hired men. Minnie, herself, was a dressmaker and her sister, Annie, a straw hat maker. The wedding took place on the 16th March, 1882 at the Priory Church. Their first child, a boy, was born in 1884 and was called Arthur. He became a gamekeeper and after short periods at Worksop Manor and Welbeck, spent most of his working life in Yorkshire. A year later, he had a sister, Lily, and the family was completed in 1890 with the birth of Daisy. As they grew to adulthood, all three children left Worksop but they kept in touch with their parents by letter and postcard. The latter was particularly significant in view of a later development of Amos Emblin's business interests.

The horse drawn vehicle parked outside the Lion Hotel was known as "town bus." It met all passenger trains that stopped at the station and carried intending patrons from there to the hotel. This photograph illustrates Amos Emblin's eye for a picture. He positioned his camera at exactly the right spot to emphasise the impressive lines of the buildings at "the top of the street."   (Photograph by permission of Richard Allsopp).

Sometime during the 1880's he left his partnership with Henry Hodges and set up on his own. He opened a draper's shop at 18, Park Street and, a little later, expanded his range of goods and changed the description of his business to that of a fancy repository. By 1892 he was advertising that, "The Wool, Toy and Fancy Repository is the best place in Worksop for 'Dukery' Views, useful and ornamental presents, etc."[1] He even went as far as claiming that his shop was, "The Oldest Toy and Fancy Repository in Worksop" which was, perhaps, something of an exaggeration. A little later, by 1894, he had transferred the drapery side of the business to a second shop at 55, Bridge Street, leaving his wife to look after the fancy repository. By another ten years both sides of his business were again conducted from the same premises at 82, Bridge Street. As with most shopkeepers at that time, this was also his home, the family living above the work place. As far as is known this was their last address in Worksop. By 1909 Amos Emblin was no longer recorded as being in business. He had been unwell during 1907 and, sometime afterwards, he and Mrs. Emblin moved to Huddersfield.

Perhaps this smart two in hand tempted Amos Emblin to take this photograph. Whether its occupant was discussing financial matters in the branch of the Sheffield Banking Company or taking refreshment at the bar of the narrow but decoratively fronted Royal Hotel, next door, will never be known. (Photograph by permission of Richard Allsopp).

If Amos Emblin had just been a Worksop shopkeeper dealing in drapery, giftware, toys and souvenirs he would hardly have merited attention a hundred years afterwards. Clearly, he had a greater claim to the notice of posterity and a clue to the reason for this is hinted in the advertisement of 1892 that has already been mentioned.[2] Among the various items that he offered for sale was a selection of views of local scenes. These included pictures of Clumber House and church, the Priory church and gatehouse and Bridge Street. He was not the only person selling such mementos. Sissons always boasted a large stock but there was one significant difference between those displayed in their Potter Street shop and those sold by Amos Emblin. He did not buy in his from an outside supplier but took the photographs and produced the pictures himself. By the turn of the century many of these were sold as postcards. Amos Emblin was not Worksop's first photographer, there was one at work in the town as early as 1869, but he was the first to take advantage of the growing demand for picture postcards, the quickest and cheapest means of communication of the day. One penny (1/2p) would buy a card, a stamp cost half that amount and delivery by the following day was virtually certain. They were, in effect, the telephones of their day. Rather than throw away the cards that they had received many people built up collections, keeping them in albums specially made for that purpose.

Not surprisingly, Mrs. Emblin despatched a regular stream of cards to her gamekeeper son Arthur at his Yorkshire home. These were supplemented by others from Lily and Daisy, his sisters, and all were carefully placed in his album. Many of them were the work of Amos Emblin, the rest of other photographers, some local, others of national firms. Fortunately the album has survived,[3] not only preserving examples of Amos Emblin's work but also, through the messages written on them, providing invaluable snippets of family biographical information.

Amos Emblin's Worksop post cards portray the town at the turn of the 20th century, several years before the more prolific output of Ezra Taylor. Although separated by so short a time, some of them show vistas and buildings that had been altered or, indeed, had disappeared before the younger photographer began work. This is their real interest and great value. Without them, people of later generations would not know what the cattle market looked like when it occupied the site of the present Arcade buildings, or the appearance of the tiny, centuries old shop on Bridge Street from which Sally Bramer sold her widely famed toffee or, indeed, the view along Priorswell Road, looking towards the earlier humped back bridge over the canal. These are some of the post cards that record bygone Worksop, scenes that have long disappeared. Others have a more contemporary look. His photograph of the new technical school and library on Watson Road [4] was one of the first taken of that building while that of Smith's mill on the canal side shows it still incomplete, encased in scaffolding. Another, with a rather futuristic look to it, features a motor bus parked outside the Town Hall.[5] Unfortunately both known copies of this card are very faded and it is impossible to see whether it was locally owned or just passing through the town.[6] So far the writer has seen twenty different Worksop post cards produced by Amos Emblin. There must have been others though their number cannot have been great. Only very occasionally are they on offer at post card fairs. However, most of them are easily recognised by the distinctive lettering of their captions. This can be clearly seen on those cards that are used as illustrations. One of Sparken Hill that lacks this marking has "A. Emblin. Photographer, Worksop" printed on the back.

Perhaps it was not surprising a hundred years ago for a shopkeeper interested in photography to supplement his stock by producing postcard views of the town in which he lived. There was, though, another side to Amos Emblin's work that is less easy to explain. As well as the cards of Worksop, his camera was also busy at Welbeck and, to a lesser extent, at Clumber and Osberton. At the former, he took a comprehensive selection of pictures, mainly of the Abbey but also some of the other buildings in the grounds. More exceptional though were group photographs taken during the royal visit of King Edward VII and Queen Alexandra in 1905. Though less exalted in status, he also photographed groups of workmen. Two that have survived are simply captioned,

"Beaters to his grace." Clearly Amos Emblin enjoyed the patronage of the Duke of Portland and was also permitted to wander the estate in search of his pictures. Sending a post card to her son, Arthur, on the 2nd, October, 1905, Mrs. Emblin wrote, "Dad has gone to Welbeck to photograph the swans ... ." Doubtless there were many such occasions when she was left to mind the shop while her husband was out with his camera.

Amos Emblin's son, Arthur, who was a gamekeeper, worked for a short time on the Welbeck estates. This may have aroused his father's interest in field sports and he took a number of photographs of shooting scenes. This one shows a group of beaters at Welbeck, posing behind some of the game that had fallen to the guns. (Photograph by permission of the Bassetlaw Museum).

Surviving cards suggest that he went most often to Welbeck, though he occasionally worked at the neighbouring estates as well. Among the photographs that he took at Clumber are several of "loaders, etc.," at a shooting party and there is a similar picture, taken at Osberton of a group of beaters. It seems most likely that such photographs were taken by prior arrangement: one where this was definitely so also concerned Osberton. Following their golden wedding in 1906, the presents received by the Rt. Hon. F.J.S. and Mrs. Foljambe were duly set out and were photographed by Mr. Emblin. The reason for such distinguished patronage is not clear. It could simply be that he was regarded as the best local photographer though there may have been other reasons, hidden by the passing years.

Whatever its cause, it was not a privilege that he enjoyed for long as, by 1907, his health had begun to fail. On the 27th March Mrs. Emblin sent a post card to her son, Arthur. "Will write tomorrow. got dad upstairs today in sitting room. he has not had his clothes on a fortnight today. I went out Saturday first time not very strong yet. Love Mother." A week later he was no better. Another card told the story. "dad eyes is bad - have to feed him (the next word is illegible) write tomorrow. Love from Mother." With her ailing husband to care for and the shop to manage these were worrying and demanding days for Mrs. Emblin. In addition to these concerns, she had another matter very much on her mind for on the 28th April, Arthur was due to marry Alice Fletcher whose father was a blacksmith at Ranby. The wedding went ahead as planned at Babworth church though it doesn't look as if Amos Emblin was well enough to attend. Writing to Mrs. Emblin after the event, the bride's mother asked, " .. we shall like to know if Mr. Emblin is any better .. " while Alice herself, on the day following her wedding, expressed the wish, "Hope Mr. Emblin is no worse."

By mid May there seemed no change. Arthur was told, "Dad not so well yesterday and this morning very low. I think he is getting sick of being indoors but his legs are so funny rubbing him with olive oil." Six weeks later there was little progress to report. On the 1st. July Mrs. Emblin wrote, "Dad been in bed all day. Not much better. Dr. says keep him out of the shop." After that despondent note, improvement set in, so much so, that on the 8th August, Amos himself wrote a card to his wife from Sheffield, "Dear M. Just got to S(heffield) raining lovley call in at BB. Love from AE." The signs are that he continued in reasonable health as, towards the end of the year, he informed Arthur, "We are thinking of killing our 2 pigs Dec 9 they will be smaller than usual. They are just about wild now." Whether these remarks imply that the pigs were not properly cared for during his illness is not clear. Mrs. Emblin's hands had been sufficiently full without worrying about them. She would certainly welcome the chance of a break and one such occurred in October, 1908.

Lily, her daughter, was living in Blackpool, probably in service, and Mrs. Emblin went to stay with her. Whether she was expecting him or not, but, while she was there Amos joined her for a few days. The rather surprised comment of Arthur, "fancy pa coming to see you," suggests that the visit had not been arranged beforehand. Not content with his visit to Blackpool, Amos Emblin moved on to spend some time with his son and daughter-in-law who were then living at Bradley Wood near Huddersfield. He gave a brief account of his journey on a post card to his wife who remained at Blackpool. "Changed at Manchester no time to waste, on to Halifax, short wait. Then to Hudd(ersfield) 1/4 past 6. no rain all day. all right. Love and best wishes. A.E."

By the time that he wrote this post card, Amos Emblin had either given up his business or was about to do so. Shortly afterwards he and his wife left Worksop and moved to Huddersfield to be near to their gamekeeper son. Whether they went to live with him is not clear but if they did, their stay could not have been long as they ultimately took up residence in The Castle, Beaumont Park, an address that was not as grand as it might sound. The park was opened in 1883 and is situated on a steep hill side site in Lockwood, a mile or so to the south of Huddersfield. It is mainly a wooded area with paths wending their way between the trees and stepped ways providing more direct progress for the energetic. The Castle stood about half way down the slope and was a place of refreshment for visitors to the park. For his final years, Amos Emblin was its proprietor. It was quite imposing in appearance, substantially built of stone. To the right was a tall, tower-like structure. Here the Emblins lived while the refreshment room stretched out to the left. Although of two storeys with ornamental parapets at both roof levels, they were lower than the tower, adding to the general castle appearance of the whole building. The ground in front was levelled and bordered with lawns and shrubs, a pleasant spot for a pot of tea on a warm summer's day. Sadly it is no longer there. It closed around forty years ago and was subsequently demolished. All that now stands is a short stretch of wall, a few feet high, and an adjoining balustrade.

Amos Emblin died on the 7th January, 1914 at his home at the Castle. He was 58 years old. The causes of his death were listed as gall stones, peritonitis and exhaustion. On the 16th January the Worksop Guardian briefly reported his death, stating that he was, "for many years resident in Worksop, being in business as a draper, ... " There was no mention of his work as a photographer and as the great majority of his post cards do not bear his name he has become virtually forgotten. This is a shame for his cards, the first to be produced locally, capture views of buildings and street scenes that would not otherwise be known. Their historical value apart, as the illustrations show, they were pictures of the highest quality. For these reasons alone, all who are interested in bygone Worksop are indebted to Amos Emblin. It is a pity that so little is known about him.

Notes and References

1. Sissons' Penny Illustrated Guide to the Dukeries, Sherwood Forest and Worksop. Undated c.1892.

2. Ibid.

3. It is held in the Bassetlaw Museum at Retford.

4. When the present library was opened in 1938, this became part of the Victoria Hospital It was demolished at the same time as the rest of the hospital buildings.

5. One is in the Cecil Brown collection in Worksop library, the other in the Emblin album in the Bassetlaw Museum.

6. Since this was written, further research has revealed that the bus was calling at Worksop on a trial run.

The Day War Broke Out.

Few, if any, Worksop people in the summer of 1914 thought that the shooting of an Austrian Archduke in the distant town of Sarajevo would have any effect on their lives. They were aware of the fact: it had been reported in the Worksop Guardian:[1] such things did happen. In the meantime they had their own lives to lead and their own troubles to contend with. For many, life was a struggle. The few shillings that they earned each week were barely enough to pay the rent, put bread on the table and a coat on their backs. Summer, however, brought its compensations. In the warm sunny weather that prevailed that year, a walk in the surrounding, unspoilt countryside cost nothing and other diversions mere coppers. On the Town Ground the cricket was good, Worksop was top of the Bassetlaw league and W.H. Copestake, mainstay of the local team for many seasons, top of the league batting averages. In early August, just across the road, at the Empire on Central Avenue, those who could afford it were promised, "The greatest combination of talent ever seen in Worksop." Undaunted by such a boast, the nearby Royal Theatre announced a combined programme of variety and films, top of the bill being The 3 Piquays, "the most wonderful upside down dancers ever seen." And if such attractions did not suit, then the Gaiety on Bridge Street featured a selection of films, "Life" and "Count Zarka" at the beginning of the week and, in view of the situation, the forbodingly titled "Facing Eternity" at the end. Even more eagerly awaited by many people than these attractions of stage and screen were the high spots of the summer, the great agricultural shows that were to be held over the bank holiday weekend, on Monday the 3rd, and Tuesday the 4th of August at Welbeck and Clumber.

Despite the rumblings of imminent war that were sounding ever louder from Central Europe, few Worksop people thought that they would be affected by any subsequent conflict. Even if they were, the local territorials were ready. From the 31st. July the Worksop men of C Squadron of the Sherwood Rangers Yeomanry were to parade four times in the succeeding five days. The first of these occasions had an ominous ring to it: the men were to wear their khaki uniforms. Little did they realise that many of them would never again ride out resplendent in their green and gold and that for the more fortunate who did, many years would pass before that happened. Meanwhile, as they practised their musketry and carried out mounted drill on the Plain Piece, their infantry fellow townsmen who made up G company of the 8th Battalion of the Notts. and Derbys. Regiment were away on their annual camp at Hunmanby near Filey. Here they drilled and marched, fired their rifles and took part in field exercises though it is doubtful if any of them saw a trench, let alone spent any time in one. This omission would be fully rectified during the months ahead.

Those who refused to believe in the seriousness of the situation or, indeed, were unaware of it, became better informed as they read their copies of the Worksop Guardian on Friday, the 31st. July. Under the headline "The Shadow of War" a speech of the previous afternoon by the Prime Minister, Mr. Herbert Asquith, in the House of Commons was reported in some detail. "They met," he said, "at a time of gravity that was almost unparalleled in the experience of everyone. The issues of peace and war were hanging in the balance, and with them the risk of a catastrophe of which it was impossible to measure either the dimension or the effects."

Such words no doubt dampened the pleasurable expectancy that many had of the forthcoming bank holiday. On the day itself, Monday, the 3rd. August, the Welbeck show went ahead as planned and, although to the outward eye, all seemed as usual, a general feeling of apprehension tempered the pleasure of the large crowd. About one thousand people sat down to the lunch and, the meal over, the Duke of Portland rose to propose the health of the king. In his preliminary words, he strove to rouse the patriotic feelings of his hearers, "At a solemn time like this when our country is threatened by the terrible menace of war," he said, "it behoves, nay, it is our bounden duty to put aside their personal opinions, their personal prejudices, and their personal conveniences....... It behoves everyone to place the good of the country and the safety of the state before everything and anything." After this stirring call to loyalty, the duke proposed the health of the king which, "The great company .... drank .... with all solemnity, and three cheers for the King, led by the Duke, were given with great enthusiasm."[2] On the following day, the 4th, interest was transferred to Clumber where a similar event took place. "The show was a very good one," reported the local paper, "but over it hung the war cloud, and European matters appeared to be more discussed than those pertaining

Tuesday, the 4th August, 1914 was warm and sunny and many Worksop people spent the time at Clumber Show, a popular annual occasion. It was to be the last for a while for later on that day Great Britain declared war on Germany. This photograph, taken a few years earlier, shows the Duke and Duchess of Newcastle examining the trophies that were to be awarded during the day.

to agriculture." For many attending the show it was to be their last peace time outing. Before the day was out, Britain was at war with Germany. "The lamps are going out all over Europe," sadly mused Sir Edward Grey, the Foreign Secretary, "we shall not see them lit again in our lifetime."

Next day, the 5th, signs of both war and peace mingled on the town's streets. Of the former, local territorials prepared for their imminent departure while of the latter, crowds flocked into town by train for a last trip round the Dukeries. Excursions arranged for later in the week were cancelled. Little business was done in the shops. Many of the owners stood at their doorways, discussing the situation with passers-by. Later in the week there was some panic buying of foodstuffs with a consequent increase in prices. This was said to be unnecessary and was considered as unpatriotic. "There is no need for panic, it was further stated,[3] "and none for a selfish abuse of the power of the long purse." As it was, flour almost doubled in price from 1s 4d (6 1/2p) "to 2s 6d. (12 1/2p) a stone and butter, sugar and bacon were also much dearer.

Royal Visit to Worksop.   Dec. 11th, 1905.—No. 2.

This is how local people were used to seeing members of the local territorial squadron of the Sherwood Rangers Yeomanry Cavalry, resplendent in their uniforms of green and gold. On the occasion of this photograph they were providing a royal escort to King Edward V11 as he was driven through the town while on a visit to Welbeck Abbey. The year was 1905 and by then only the northern part of the Arcade had been completed.

Throughout the town the bustle of wartime preparations proceeded. The two hundred and eight members of the National Reserve were asked to volunteer for overseas service, if required and sixty five complied. Almost one hundred horses were commandeered for military service. Mr. H. Moore, local veterinary surgeon, had a busy time checking that they were fit for so drastic a change of employment. Some were provided by the posting proprietors while twenty five came from the stables at Welbeck. That the horse's fighting days might be more in the past was suggested by gestures made by two Worksop men. Mr. Henry Senior of Carlton Road offered both his car and himself for military service while Mr. Archibald Hatfield, also of Carlton Road, volunteered as a despatch rider, using his own motor cycle. Such instances do, perhaps, imply a touch of naivety and this is further illustrated by a conversation that was overheard outside the Post Office on Newcastle Avenue. A member of the National Reserve who had volunteered for overseas service was talking to a local insurance agent. "If I should get shot, old man, you won't forget to pay the wife, will you?" said the former. The agent promised that he would not and they shook hands. After chatting about the war for a few minutes the man sought additional assurance. Offering his hand again, he said, 'Put it there, old chap, and don't forget." "No, I won't. I will do so within a few minutes of receiving the notification from the War Office," was the reply, to which was added further comforting words, "Still you must not go away with any idea in your mind that you will get injured." It would be difficult to imagine such a discussion taking place once the full horrors of war were realised and weekly casualty lists occupied a prominent place in the Worksop Guardian. Perhaps the editor was a little more percipient than many when he wrote in its first wartime edition, "The struggle will be bitter and may be prolonged. We enter upon it as a United Nation, with gallant allies and whatever sacrifices may be necessary, we do not doubt that they will be made."[4]

An early sacrifice experienced by many Worksop families was separation from their loved ones as members of the local yeomanry and infantry units reported to the Shaw

Trooper Wilfred Aucock was a long serving member of the Sherwood Rangers Yeomanry. He volunteered for overseas service in the Boer War and was still in the ranks when the Great War broke out in 1914. No longer dressed for peace time duties, he is wearing the khaki uniform of active service and is equipped for war with rifle and bayonet and cavalry sabre. (Photograph by permission of Mrs. E. Greaves).

Street drill hall on that first Wednesday morning. Within all was, "bustle and orderly confusion," while outside "a huge crowd" of mothers, wives and children gathered for a last glimpse of their sons, husbands and fathers before they left town. As a preliminary all the men were medically examined, the yeomanry by Dr. Wallis and the foot soldiers by Dr. Montague. All save three were pronounced fit, and two of these with defective teeth accepted the government offer of £5 to have dentures fitted so that they could rejoin their friends. One of the oldest on parade was Pioneer Sergt. W. Johnson who had served twelve years with the regulars and twenty four with the territorials. Brothers G., Tom and Ted Powell stood shoulder to shoulder while a fourth member of the same family, John, was already serving with the Coldstream Guards.

Medicals completed, the Yeomanry marched to the Catholic school on Park Street where, for the next five nights, they slept on straw mattresses with two blankets. Meals were provided at the Golden Ball. Their days were occupied with routine activities: foot drill on the field behind the school, rifle and kit inspections and a session at the swimming baths as a highlight. They were dismissed at 21.30 and lights out was sounded half an hour later. On Sunday they held a mounted parade and on the following day, in the early afternoon, they departed for Retford where they joined the rest of the regiment. As they left Worksop, over a hundred strong, they were given "a very hearty send-off by a considerable crowd in the vicinity of the Market place and the streets were lined with well-wishers."[5] With their departure the town seemed very empty for the men of G. Company of the Notts, and Derby Regiment had already left.

After two days at the drill hall, early on Friday morning they marched to the station to catch a train to Newark, each man carrying, as part of his kit, a note book and pencil, a clasp knife, a length of stout string, shaving tackle, soap, towels, a tooth brush, a hair brush and comb, a pot of vaseline and basic cutlery. The station was crowded with relations and friends and while the men, "were calm and even cheerful," many who packed the platform, "broke down repeatedly and sobbed." Within three days the pick of the town's menfolk had left, many never to return. Of the three Powell brothers, one, sadly, was lost. Compared with some families, that might be considered fortunate.

Having waved farewell and dried their eyes, the women of the town did not sit idly down to await events. A meeting was called at 5 pm on Monday, the 10th August at the Town Hall for, "Women Helpers, desirous of assisting their country in time of War." The Duchess of Newcastle promised to preside. The meeting was most encouragingly supported: the Town Hall was packed and at its end over three hundred ladies offered to make clothing and another ninety volunteered for an ambulance section. Needles were soon busy as Mr. D.J. Smith of the Beehive Stores gave a roll of flannel for them to make a start on. It was hoped that other traders would follow his example. Some ladies gave money so that more material could be bought and on Thursday afternoon, it was reported, "a large gathering of the needlework section," was busy at the Town Hall.[6] Whether the clothing that was produced was for military or civilian use is not clear.

Perhaps both categories were catered for: knitted items for the troops and general articles of clothing for such needy people as the Belgian refugees.

Local government was not as quick off the mark as the town's ladies and it was not until Monday, the 17th August that the Urban District Council met. The chairman, Mr. P.S. Whittell, "referred to the desirability of making preparations with regard to what might be great distress in the town."[7] Just what form this distress might take is not clear. Worksop was too far from the coast to fear naval bombardment and attack from the air was as yet unknown. However, there was a real fear of invasion and much was subsequently made of this in recruiting campaigns so perhaps the chairman had that in mind when making his remarks. He went on to say that the council had been asked by the Local Government Board to form a committee to administer any grants that might be received from the National Relief Committee. He added that he had also received a telegram from the Prince of Wales asking him to launch an appeal for donations to the National Relief Fund. This he did and the town responded generously. Contributions flowed in both from individuals and organisations. The choir of the Wesleyan church sent £3 to the fund and £2 to the Belgian Relief Fund; money that had been put aside for their annual treat while a special collection in the church realised £10 - 3s - 7d. (£10.18). The Congregationalists planned a similar collection on the 13th of September. By then £2,118 had already been raised.[8]

Young people, too, were encouraged to play their part in the war effort. Boys between 14 and 18 were urged to join the Boy Scouts where they would receive training that would enable them to be of some assistance. It was suggested that they might help gather in the harvest, taking the places of men who had already enlisted. Of far greater urgency, however, in those early days was persuading a sufficient number of men to volunteer for military service. The regular army was small and even when supplemented by reservists and the territorials, still did not compare in numbers with the large continental powers. Lord Kitchener, the Secretary of State for War, appealed for one hundred thousand men to come forward and join the colours.

Those in Worksop were not slow in responding. A recruiting office was opened on Tuesday, the 18th August at the drill hall and by the Thursday evening eighty five men had signed on. This may seem a very reasonable number but it was not regarded as good enough. Taking advantage of his position as Chairman of the Bench, Colonel Mellish of Hodsock Priory, urged everyone present at the court on the 19th August to make it widely known that there was a recruiting office in the town. Supplementing word of mouth, both local regiments appealed for recruits through the Worksop Guardian, An advertisement in the issue of the 4th September informed readers that the Sherwood Rangers Yeomanry "Fourth Oldest Yeomanry Regiment" had volunteered for foreign service and, "is now recruiting further strength." It continued, "Recruits who can ride and shoot and will volunteer for foreign service wanted immediately." Lt. Col. G.S. Foljambe who commanded the depot of the 8th Battalion of the Sherwood Foresters which was at Newark informed readers that all the officers and 82.5% of the men had volunteered for overseas service but that one hundred and seventy men were still required to bring the unit up to strength. He added, "Ex service and single men between 19 - 35 being preferred."

Like every town and village in the land, Worksop suffered its share of casualties in the war. Private Tom Lamb enlisted early in the conflict, was soon on the Western Front and was badly wounded. On this photograph, on the way to recovery, he is in the bed on the left of this picture.   (Photograph by permission of Mr. H. Lamb).

The church added its voice in this call to service, the Bishop of Southwell writing, "Ere it is too late let our young men in town and village come forward to take their part in this noble effort."[9] He regretted his inability to do more than give the call but did offer to attend meetings to encourage recruitment. A further letter on the same subject was written by Captain F. Vernon Willey of Blyth who was serving with the Sherwood Rangers. Its tone was critical rather than persuasive. He stated that, "Loafers and luggards [10] of high and low station are still to be seen," and suggested that employers should give their workers between 19 and 30 the choice of enlistment or the sack. "No man under 30," he added, "is indispensable at home, when his country needs his services for war."

In view of these sentiments it is surprising to read, "recruiting has been remarkably satisfactory." In the first month of the war, about five hundred men had responded to the country's call. If the reservists, territorials and yeomanry were added, the number of young men at arms must have been about eight hundred. Captain Willey would have been pleased to know that "loafers and laggards" were in a minority in Worksop. Recruiting was no doubt helped when the office was moved from the out of the way Shaw Street to the more centrally situated Town Hall where, it was reported, "Col. the Hon. C.H. Willoughby and his hard working energetic staff have been busily engaged."

Good as this might seem, it was felt that even more men might be induced to enlist. Accordingly, on the evening of Wednesday, the 2nd, September, a mass meeting was arranged in the Empire Theatre which stood on the corner of Central Avenue with Hardy Street. So great was the throng that attended that all could not be seated. Union Jacks decked the hall and the theatre orchestra played patriotic tunes as the platform party was awaited. Just before they took their places the National Anthem was sung and three cheers given for the king. As the echoes resounded the Duke and Duchess of Portland, the Duke and Duchess of Newcastle, Sir John Robinson, Canon G.J.A. d'Arcy, Vicar of Worksop and the principal townsmen mounted the stage. The Duke of Portland was both chairman and leading speaker. He began by saying that although three thousand five hundred men in the county had already volunteered for army service, this was by no means enough. To those young men who were still at home he put the question, "Why are you loafing about doing nothing when your country is in this terrible danger? Why have you not answered Lord Kitchener's call?" The reason, he suggested, was not lack of bravery or patriotism but a failure to appreciate the danger in which the country stood. This danger, he went on to explain was nothing less than invasion and its consequent horrors. "Wake up to your duty now," the duke concluded, "wake up, while there is time; wake up, before the German host is upon us." Whether the duke had any evidence to back up so alarmist a statement, or whether he thought that a little scaremongering was justified to stimulate recruiting will perhaps never be known though the result is. At the conclusion of the meeting a good number of men indicated that they were prepared to enlist.

At the end of the first month of war the town had a strange, empty look to it, especially in the evenings and at week ends when, previously, work done, young men tended to be seen on the streets. Around eight hundred of them were away from home, undergoing the rigours of army life, preparatory to being sent to the western front. In the meantime, those still at home were invited to learn to use a rifle on the miniature range at the drill hall. Anyone wanting to take advantage of this offer could go along on three evenings of the week where they would be given necessary instruction and ammunition was free. These sessions were arranged by the Worksop detachment of the National Reserve. This seems to have been a body of men who, in the main, were too old for overseas service but who would be called upon in the event of invasion, a forerunner of the Home Guard of World War 2.

For most people, however, it was a matter of keeping the home fires burning, awaiting a letter from the loved one whose photograph occupied a proud place on the mantelpiece and, perhaps, from time to time, making up a parcel of items that

Worksop not only erected a memorial to commemorate its dead, it also built a new road to place it on. It was not until 1928 that both were ready when, on the 9th July of that year, King George V and Queen Mary drove along the newly laid out Memorial Avenue to officially open it. This photograph was taken a little prior to that event. The memorial is complete but the road still has to be surfaced.

it was hoped would ease the hardship of military life. For any who were in doubt as to what to put into such packages, the War Office, through the Official Press Bureau, made a number of suggestions. Some of these would no doubt be most acceptable, others merely useful and included, "handkerchiefs, bootlaces, newspapers, periodicals, chocolate, peppermints, dried fruits, briar pipe and tobacco pouches (tobacco packed in thick tinfoil, if possible), cigarettes, cigarette papers and cigarette tobacco, small tins of boracic ointment or borated vaseline for sore feet, pocket knives, post cards and lead pencils".[11]

Probably missed by many readers, tucked away at the bottom of a column of The Worksop Guardian [12] was a brief news item that was a portent of more ominous tidings to come. It recorded Worksop's first casualties of the war. Lieutenant E.W.S. Foljambe of Osberton Hall, serving in the Rifle Brigade, was reported wounded and missing. It was subsequently discovered that he was a prisoner of war. Private Robinson of Kilton Road was wounded in the hands by shrapnel. No more details were given. Before too long such information could not be hidden away: its volume ensured it prominence.

The war which had taken most people by surprise in the sunny days of August 1914 was to last for more than four years. For Worksop people it brought its share of restrictions and privations. These could be borne: they were but temporary inconveniences. It was the thought of the dead and the sight of the maimed, the disfigured and the permanently handicapped that remained long in the memory. Ten years elapsed before that loss was given a permanent expression in the town. On the 9th July, 1928 King George V and Queen Mary drove along a newly laid out road, thereby officially opening it. It was called Memorial Avenue and mid-way along its length stood the war memorial, upon which were inscribed the names of the fallen.

Notes and References

1. The Worksop Guardian, 3 July, 1914.
2. Ibid. 7 August, 1914.
3. Ibid.
4. Ibid.
5. Ibid. 14 August, 1914.
6. Ibid. 21 August, 1914.
7. Ibid.
8. Ibid. 11 September, 1914.
9. Ibid. 4 September, 1914.
10. Probably a printing error for laggards.
11. The Worksop Guardian, 4 September, 1914.
12. 11 September, 1914.

William and Walter.
The Straw Brothers of Worksop.

"Give me a boy until he is seven and I will give you the man," so, it is said, was the claim of the Jesuits. In a more general application such an assertion could account for the mode of life followed by William and Walter Straw, bachelor brothers, whose home at 7, Blyth Grove is now one of the more unusual properties in the care of the National Trust.

The tall, three storey building on the right of the picture, standing on the edge of the Market Place was the home and shop of David Winks, the town's principal butcher. It stood just opposite the White Hart Inn - its sign is clearly visible - and the premises of William Straw, grocer. After a period of "walking out" together, William married Florence, daughter of Mr. and Mrs. Winks and their sons, William and Walter were born in 1898 and 1899. This photograph, taken in the 1900's, shows a familiar scene of their boyhood days. (Photograph by permission of Richard Allsopp).

William Straw, senior, came to Worksop in the late 19th century from his native Sutton-in-Ashfield and set up in business as a grocer and seed merchant in a shop at the top of Bridge Street, facing the market. Almost opposite, one of an isolated group of buildings that stood on the edge of the market itself, was the home and butcher's shop of David Winks. Not surprisingly, living in such proximity, the two families became friendly and in 1896, in the town's Priory Church, William Straw married Florence, the butcher's daughter. As was then customary, the couple made their home above the shop, gradually assembling the furniture and fittings that they were later to move to Blyth Grove and which can now be seen by visitors to that house. It would be a happy thought that the child's Windsor chair, a product of the workshop of local chairmaker William Gilling and which was bought in 1869 by Mr. and Mrs. Winks for Florence was moved across the road during the early years of the marriage as there was soon a suitable occupant for it. The couple's first child was born in 1898; a boy, named William after his father. Before the next year was out he had a brother, Walter, who bore as a second name that of his maternal grandfather, Winks. A third boy, David, lived but briefly and did not survive infancy.

This photograph of Mr. and Mrs. Straw and their sons William and Walter was taken in 1910 in the yard at the back of the shop and family home on the Market Place. The horse, used to pulling the shop delivery vehicle, would not feel overburdened as both boys were small in stature and light in weight. (Photograph by permission of Roz and Ian Davies)

Though born just before the turn of the century, the boys grew up during Edwardian times and there is no doubt that for them they were idyllic days. Home was both loving and secure: nothing that was needful was lacking though thrift - some would say parsimony - rather than indulgence was a guiding principle. If a household article was sound, it wasn't replaced: if some innovatory item wasn't strictly necessary, it wasn't acquired. William Straw would rather see his sovereigns in the bank than in the tills of his fellow shopkeepers. This attitude of careful spending, even frugality, was not lost on the boys, Though they didn't deny themselves anything that they wanted, they never wanted many of the things that other families deemed essential. In old age, Walter recalled an instance of their father's influence on their own outlook. "When the wireless set was invented," he told the writer, "father said, 'Well, I suppose it's all right for people who are ill or who can't read, but I don't think we need one', "And" he added, "we've never thought to disagree with him."

Supplementing these domestic influences were those of the house across the road and especially of their grandfather, David W. Winks. He was a Worksopian to the core who loved the town, its people and its traditions: his memory was a storehouse of stories, incidents and escapades of its immediate past and these he poured out to the two boys. They proved eager listeners and retained life-long recollections of all they heard. William later wrote down much of this information, adding to it the results of his own researches into the town's past. As well as his work in the butcher's shop, David Winks played his part in town affairs. He served his turn as churchwarden at the Priory church and also sat for a time on the Local Board of Health.

There is no doubt that he was a well known and popular figure in the town though perhaps there was a little exaggeration in Walter's comment that, "Grandfather could leave his shop on the market and walk to the Common End (Victoria Square) and he would know everyone he saw." In 1909, when an old man, as a mark of their respect and affection, his family commissioned Charles E. Baldock, a noted local artist and grandson of the even more highly regarded James W. Baldock, to paint his portrait. It now hangs in the sitting room of the house on Blyth Grove and shows an elderly gentleman of benign appearance with perhaps just the suggestion of a quizzical if not a mischievous turn to his mouth. One senses that laughter was rarely long absent when grandfather Winks was telling his tales of old Worksop.

This interest in and love of Worksop, engendered at their grandfather's knee, never left the boys; William, in his time becoming the acknowledged authority on the town's past while Walter's interest widened to include local archaeology. Meanwhile their formal education took place at the Abbey Boys' school in Worksop and the King Edward VI Grammar School at Retford. The premises of the former on Potter Street were fairly new, having been built in 1877. Prior to that the large upstairs room in the Priory Gatehouse had been used. The Abbey Boys' School was maintained by the church and enjoyed a reputation in the town for giving its pupils a sound, if basic education. Supplementing this somewhat formal fare, the school had a little library for the boys' use as well as a display cabinet for museum items while in the playground some pieces of gymnastic apparatus had been set up which had been acquired in 1878 on the closure of the Pestalozzian School in the town. William, in particular, recalled a set of parallel bars which the boys called "dodging poles."

School work posed few problems for the two brothers and each one, in due course, transferred to the grammar school at Retford, then under the stern and rigorous headmastership of the Revd. Thomas Gough. With around one hundred and twenty boys on its roll, the school was noted for its industry and learning. These attributes were not merely encouraged, they were demanded and backsliders could expect to experience the wrath of Mr. Gough who was never loath to spoil the child through any reluctance to spare the rod. Not that William and Walter needed to fear such chastisement: they were both conscientious by nature though their days at the grammar school must have reinforced this attitude to work and duty.

Never the less, as they stood on the platform of Worksop station, awaiting the Great Central Railway train that would carry them to Retford, they may well have felt some qualms at what their hours at school might bring. Occasionally, however, they may have been able to raise their noses from the seemingly unremitting grindstone. Though the second master, Mr. Arthur Kidson, taught maths, and though he was no more averse to use the cane than Mr. Gough, he was a man of wide interests and these he sought to share with his pupils in opportune moments. One of them was local history and in 1905 he had published a history of East Retford parish church. Any snippets of information on that subject that fell from his lips when either of the Straw boys was in his class would have brightened their day, have been snapped up and committed to memory.

Each Sunday the Straw family attended worship at Worksop Priory Church where, until 1909 the vicar was the Revd. Henry T. Slodden. Of imposing presence, he was neither "High" nor "Low" in churchmanship but always strove to conduct a dignified service rather than one that was severely plain or over ornate. This proved yet another influence that determined life-long attitudes in the boys. A traditional service according to the Prayer Book with readings from the Authorized Version of the Bible were, for them, essentials for Sunday worship and it was a very sad day when, in old age, the introduction of more modern trends at St. John's church where they were then members, made them feel no longer able to attend. Though they were probably unaware of it at the time, Mr. Slodden had little time for anything modern, preferring the way of life and, wherever possible, using the articles of his younger days. It was said that he always wrote with a quill pen in his correspondence and when preparing his sermons while, in 1902, at the opening of a new library building, he roundly condemned modern novels as, "neurotic, erotic and tommy-rotic." Something of this attitude may have rubbed off on the Straw boys for they, too, had little use for anything of new design or innovative of purpose. It would have been interesting to have heard William's comments when Walter bought a camera to record his archaeological work. Unfortunately these are not known.

Like most shopkeeping families of the time, the Straws lived over their business premises. Doubtless such homes could be made quite comfortable and the convenience of being on the spot was both time saving and a means of security. There were, however, disadvantages. They were cramped externally, there was no escape from the street noises and there was no space for a garden. These first two conditions were unavoidable: for the third there was an alternative. As in many towns, allotments were available. Most of these were cultivated in the traditional way to produce vegetables but one area was somewhat different. Situated off Park Street and known as the "gentlemen's gardens," tenancy was restricted to business men who traded on Bridge Street, the town's main shopping thoroughfare. While vegetables were certainly grown, they occupied but part of the plots as most gardens also had a well trimmed lawn, were brightened with flowers and bordered with a low, neatly clipped hedge. Instead of the more usual nondescript allotment shed, many of the gentlemen's gardens boasted a small summer house for, despite their masculine name, they were places of resort for the whole family.

On Thursday afternoons, that was early closing day, when the weather invited, Mr. and Mrs. Straw walked the few hundred yards to the garden, he to attend to its cultivation, she to sit in the shade and occupy herself with her needle. Around four o'clock they were joined by the two boys, eager to share a picnic tea with their parents. Similar scenes prevailed in the other gardens. For those habitually cooped up in shop or kitchen, beset with the worries of business or domestic trials, they were temporary havens of tranquillity. It was there that William and Walter developed their proficiency at and great love for gardening. Until old age and infirmity made it impossible they continued to ply their spade, rake and hoe though by then the gentlemen's gardens were much changed in appearance and status. Today, levelled by the bulldozer, new housing has replaced the allotments: the brothers would not approve.

Attractive window dressing was not a skill practised by Mr. William Straw, as is shown in this photograph of him with his two sons standing in the shop doorway. Although it would not be approved nowadays, it was then quite usual to display such goods as sides of bacon and hams out of doors despite all risks of contamination. (Picture by permission of Roz and Ian Davies).

By the time the country mourned the death of King Edward VII, the future outlook on life of William and Walter Straw had been moulded by the circumstances, the personalities and the values of their early years. Unlike many people, they held fast to these influences and looked back, albeit through rose-tinted spectacles, to Edwardian days as an idyllic time, one to be preserved in their own lives and immediate surroundings, even though the world around them was racing on at a much faster pace. Time, however, refused to stand still. The boys grew up and as the Great War drew its grim and relentless curtain on the happy and settled days of their childhood, decisions had to be made on their future. William, a quiet, rather retiring young man of academic inclinations was to continue his education at university while Walter, who had a more open disposition, was to tie on the grocer's apron and help in the shop. Such arrangements were interrupted awhile as, like all their contemporaries, both brothers experienced a short period of army service. That completed, William attended London University where he studied English literature, ultimately gaining his M.A. Thus qualified, he took a teaching appointment at the City of London College. He would certainly be a thorough teacher:

whether he enjoyed his work is perhaps doubtful; term time exile in London being made a little more bearable by the regular receipt of letters from home and the weekly arrival of the Worksop Guardian. Posted "hot from the press" and because of the greater frequency of deliveries in those days this reached him on Thursday evening. Meanwhile, in Worksop, people had to wait until Friday morning before they could buy a copy.

When William Straw, senior, and Florence Winks married in 1896 and set up home above the shop they were following normal practice though, by then, there were a few exceptions. It is generally believed that William Middleton, a draper with premises on Bridge Street, was the first business man to move away from his shop though he didn't go very far. His new home, "Birkland Villa," built by his cousin George Gregg, where the United Reformed church now stands, was not more than two minutes walk from his place of work. Others moved further afield, tempted from the bustle and noise of the main streets to the greater tranquillity and spaciousness of the newly developed roads and avenues on the outskirts of the town.

This is what today we would call a "flyer" for the grocer's shop of William Straw. It most likely appeared in the Guardian and possibly in any local directory for this area.

The shop is still there, the outside little changed, but the inside has been transformed into "Mr. Straw's Café." (Photo by permission of Richard Allsopp).

Blyth Grove was one such street. The first of its large villa-like houses was built in 1905 and it soon became a most desirable address for professional and well to do business men. Though mainly detached, there was one pair of semi-detached houses and when one of these, number 7, became vacant in the early 1920's, it was bought by William Straw. The family didn't move in straight away as the house was first decorated throughout at a cost of £100. This proved money well spent for neither lick of paint nor roll of wallpaper was applied during the entire period of the Straw's occupancy. By 1923 the family had settled into their new home, their furniture and household goods, long familiar to them in the rooms over the shop, giving it a welcome, lived in appearance. Rarely did either generation of the Straws see fit to buy any new piece of furniture: if an article continued to fulfil its purpose, it wasn't replaced. The dictates of fashion had no place in their lives.

Thus, the items that present day visitors see will mainly be such as would be found in middling class homes of the 1890's and turn of the century years. There is nothing to make the lover of antiques drool though several pieces are of interest. One is a long case clock that stands on the stairs and bears the maker's name of George Stacey of Worksop while at least two of the chairs were products of the town's chairmakers. On the walls too, among the plethora of pictures, prints, photographs and ephemera that hang there, are one or two with local associations. The portrait of David Winks by Charles Baldock has already been mentioned. There is also at least one painting, a pleasant rural scene, by his more distinguished grandfather, James Walsham Baldock.

Once decorated, furnished and embellished, the Straw family settled in to their new home and, as was their wont, made little alteration or addition to its initial layout. Neither invention nor innovation interested them. Radio, television, the telephone, the refrigerator passed them by as if they had never been devised. Within their own world of their home, the shop, their gardens, church and personal interests, their lives were full, content and even happy. Routine was breached just once a year when the family took a holiday at Scarborough, always staying at the same hotel.

The 27th June, 1932 forced a change on this seemingly settled and ordered way of life. On that day William Straw, senior, died while working on his allotment in the gentlemen's gardens. He was 67 years old. An immediate result of this was that Walter took charge of the shop. This presented no difficulty. His apprenticeship had been long and he had become an astute business man: he would carry on in the manner to which he was accustomed. Within the home, too, as little was changed as possible. Mr. Straw's clothes remained on hooks in the hall or stored in drawers, his pipes and tobacco were left ready to hand. It was almost as if the dead man was expected to return at any minute and resume the life that had ended. The embalming of 7, Blyth Grove had begun. Explanations for this can only be tentative. Great love for a husband and father certainly contributed and there may also have been an initial feeling of "waste not, want not" too. Father and sons were of similar height and stature, clothes bought for the former would certainly have fitted the latter. Whatever the reasons they were given further expression seven years later when, on the 8th November, 1939 Mrs. Straw died at the age of 75.

William, who, a year earlier, had given up his work in London, returned home to keep house. He soon settled to a domestic routine, dividing his time between the house, the garden, his books and his research into local history. Following the outbreak of war, he worked on a cousin's farm at Babworth and, as he later admitted, enjoyed his time there; probably more than his years in the classroom. In fact, it is doubtful if he missed the teaching, or the activities and the society of the school. The more private of the brothers, he never sought company though he did not completely cut himself off from it. For many years he was constant in his attendance at St. John's Church, serving on the parochial church council and as churchwarden.

The Straw family must have felt that they were going up in the world when, in the early 1920's, Mr. William Straw bought no. 7 Blyth Grove, a semi-detached villa in a very desirable part of the town. It is the house on the right of the picture. After it had been completely re-decorated, the family took up residence in 1923. It was to be William and Walter's home for the rest of their lives. Now, looked after by the National Trust, it is visited by thousands of people every year.

He was also co-opted to the library committee of the Worksop Borough Council and was regularly applied to when information on local historical matters was needed. Some of his replies to these queries, replete with detail, are still held in the library's files. There is no doubt that William Straw's knowledge of Worksop, its history and its people was greater than that of any of his contemporaries and the regret must be expressed that he never shared it more widely. His only publication was a book to mark the centenary of St. John's church. It was a detailed, scholarly work, as was to be expected, but limited in scope and only made the reader wish that he had cast his net wider and produced a more general study of the town. That would, indeed, have been a treasure trove.

Reflecting further this interest, William was a life member of the Thoroton Society. He was not particularly active though enjoyed spending an hour or two in the Society's room on his twice yearly visits to Nottingham. Both he and Walter invariably occupied front row seats at the Society's occasional lectures at Worksop and, at their end, during question time, William usually offered an apposite gem of knowledge from his life-long studies. The accessibility of local footpaths was another of his concerns and woe betide the person who attempted to impede or deny this.

Walter was a little more genial than his brother as, indeed, he needed to be in his daily work in the shop. While sharing many of William's interests, he was also a member of the town's Chamber of Trade. In fact, two of the most surprising items in the house may derive from this involvement. One is a receipt for a fee for a correspondence course in ballroom dancing from the Arthur Murray school: the other a suit bearing the label of Gerald Lant, bespoke tailor, who had left wartime London and set up business in Worksop, quite close to the Straw's shop. Doubtless Walter wore the suit at important Chamber functions though whether he sufficiently mastered the terpsichorean skills to take to the floor with any confidence is perhaps unlikely.

For thirty or more years, from the time of their mother's death, the brothers were familiar and regular sights on the streets of Worksop. Walter was the first to appear as he made his daily way to the shop, firstly on foot, latterly by van. He was followed by William, his flat cap, old raincoat and Wellingtons belying both his learning and his wealth. Calling at W.H. Smith's for his copy of the Times, he continued to the gentlemen's gardens where he put in a stint with spade and fork before returning home to prepare the mid-day meal. Thereafter he was usually occupied about the house, Saturday afternoons being a little special when, towards tea time, he made preparations to bake bread for the forthcoming week. It was on Sunday, however, that the brothers etched their presence on many memories. Immaculate in bowler hats, black jackets and black pin-striped trousers and carrying rolled umbrellas they made their way to and from morning service at St. John's Church, a place of worship that they attended, served and loved for many years. After Sunday dinner, their bowlers replaced by the more casual homburg or trilby, they set out on a five mile perambulation of the town. Their route, timing and theme of conversation never varied. As they made their way along familiar streets and round by the gentlemen's gardens, their comments were on the changes that had taken place in their lifetimes: changes in which they could see little that was good or beneficial.

Their way of life continued unchanged until the 1970's. Early in the decade Walter gave up the shop. Typical of the man, though wanting to dispose of the stock, he refused to reduce any price by as much as a penny. The result was that many items, some of them quite old, were taken to Blyth Grove and stored away in any available place there. Walter's retirement was short. On the 16th December, 1976 he died at the age of 77. Few who were present at the funeral will forget the sight of William; shrunken in stature, sad of countenance and, above all, a picture of utter loneliness. For almost ten years he carried on, as far as was possible, in his habitual way until, in 1985 infirmity took its toll and he had to go into hospital. There he remained until his death on the 3rd. December 1990 when he was 92. All the family were buried in the same grave: father, mother, infant son David, Walter and, finally, William. Inscribed beneath his name and the dates of his life was the one word, "Re-united."

Only a few people had entered 7 Blyth Grove during the brothers' lifetime so its condition and contents were as great a surprise to most as was the amount of money, around one and a half million pounds, that William bequeathed to the National Trust. Local comment that the brothers had amassed such a sum because they never spent anything was, in essence, true though not to the extent that they denied themselves anything that they felt was essential. Few Worksop people spent as much on books as William, as his extensive collection gives proof. That both he and Walter retained the habit of thrift ingrained into their personalities from childhood, that they preferred to live out their days in an Edwardian ambience and surround themselves with visible and tangible reminders of their deceased parents certainly suggests a degree of the unusual, if not a touch of eccentricity in their make up. Those who knew them well, however, will remember them with affection as they recall the pleasure and interest of their company and bring to mind their various idiosyncrasies and the many stories of their sayings and doings. Of these, just one must suffice. After a break in at St. John's Church Institute, the parochial church council were discussing remedial measures. To replace the door that had been damaged in gaining entry, it was proposed that a joiner be commissioned to make and fit a new one. Walter didn't agree. "I suggest," he said, "that we look for a suitable second hand door and then see if we've got someone in the congregation who can fix it."

It is doubtful if William ever envisaged the outcome of his generosity to the National Trust. That it decided to restore down to the smallest detail the home that he and Walter shared for so many years would certainly have pleased him, though it is extremely unlikely that he would have approved the admission of the general public. Relatively few crossed its threshold during his lifetime; that over seven thousand should have wandered through its rooms and peered at its contents within four months of its opening would have appalled him. He would have been similarly saddened by the fate of the gentlemen's gardens. What would have brought the brothers a degree of pleasure was the publicity that William's bequest brought to Worksop, the town of their birth and the greater part of their lives; the town that they knew and loved, especially of their recollections of it in their youthful days that they strove to preserve in their memories, their ways and in their home.

Walter and William:
Bound for church.

INDEX